Underst
Organizational Sustainability
through African Proverbs

Praise for this book

'The power of the story is gaining renewed recognition in development practice, as the universal truths and local texture of traditional proverbs and fables strike a chord with people – whether in the village or the presidential palace – and this is a significant tool for agents of change. This richly textured book gives a fresh insight into how African proverbs can be used to communicate and inform organizational change. In the age of the workshop and project logframe we need to remember and come back to the interaction around stories – to the fireside illustrations and instructive "aha" of a good proverb as it sheds light on our human process and character. A proverb is worth a hundred PowerPoint slides.'

Jackie Davies, Founder, Communication for Development Network

'Anyone concerned with the practice of organizational development internationally should read this book as it offers an alternative and fresh perspective on organizational change rooted in African culture and experience.'

Professor John Hailey, Cass Business School, City University, London

'The leadership wisdom contained in this book is essential reading. It expands the depth and breadth of African proverbial use and skilfully guides leaders around the world on how to get the best from their people and organizations.'

Afia Zakiya, Country Representative, WaterAid Ghana

'Wisdom for daily living in Africa was passed on to new generations through proverbs and folktales. This book elevates this wisdom to a new level by showing how indigenous African proverbs can be used to improve the performance of modern organizations everywhere.'
Monica Kapiriri, author of Sleeping Giant: Unleashing Africa's Potential

'In our delivery of leadership training for hundreds of African women in agricultural research and development, we have had to borrow many ideas from the West. Thanks to this new edition of *Understanding Organizational Sustainability through African Proverbs*, African women will build their confidence and become more strategic leaders. What these authors have provided is of immediate relevance.'

Vicki Wilde, Director, African Women in Agricultural Research and Development (AWARD), Nairobi

Understanding Organizational Sustainability through African Proverbs

Insights for leaders and facilitators

Chiku Malunga
with Charles Banda

Foreword by Alan Fowler

PRACTICAL ACTION
Publishing

Practical Action Publishing
The Schumacher Centre
Bourton on Dunsmore, Rugby,
Warwickshire, CV23 9QZ, UK
www.practicalactionpublishing.org

First published by Impact Alliance Press 2004
Practical Action Publishing edition 2013

ISBN 978-1-85339-652-6 Paperback
ISBN 978-1-85339-759-2 Hardback
ISBN 978-1-78044-652-3 Ebook
ISBN 978-1-78044-759-9 Library Ebook

Book DOI: http://dx.doi.org/10.3362/9781780447599

Malunga, Chiku (2013) *Understanding Organizational Sustainability
through African Proverbs: Insights for Leaders and Facilitators*,
Rugby, UK: Practical Action Publishing.

Since 1974, Practical Action Publishing has published and
disseminated books and information in support of international
development work throughout the world. Practical Action
Publishing is a trading name of Practical Action Publishing Ltd
(Company Reg. No. 1159018), the wholly owned publishing
company of Practical Action. Practical Action Publishing trades
only in support of its parent charity objectives and any profits are
covenanted back to Practical Action (Charity Reg. No. 247257,
Group VAT Registration No. 880 9924 76).

Cover design by Practical Action Publishing
Typeset by Practical Action Publishing
Printed in the United Kingdom

We dedicate this book to all the people who believe in development, especially the development of Africa. We also dedicate it to all the sons and daughters of Africa in diaspora. We believe it will offer them a means to reconnect with their roots in mother Africa.

Contents

http://dx.doi.org/10.3362/9781780447599.000

        What is an organizational assessment?   65
        The purpose of an organizational assessment   66
        The benefits of a self-assessment   66
        The organizational self-assessment process   67
        First-hand lessons for using African proverbs in OD work 68
        Factors hindering effective use of organizational
            assessments   70

    Appendix: Sample diagnostic instruments   73
        Proverbs self-assessment tool for organizations   73
        Self-reflection tool for leaders   79
        Self-reflection tool for consultants   81

    References   83

Foreword

Good books about organizations – how to understand and help change them – need at least two elements. One is rootedness in proven practice. The other is a reflection on practice that moves beyond time and place to unearth and explore deeper principles that merit and provoke reflection by others. With this in mind, in reading this book I was struck by the powerful way in which African proverbs not only unite these essential elements but, because they express an accumulated wisdom of human relations, add dimensions to practice in ways that are soulful, respectful, practical and socially embedded.

Chiku Malunga's insightful and creative way of combining the profound with practical stands out as a distinctive quality of his own reflection that has caused me to rethink what I thought I knew. I hope and believe that it will have a similar affect on all its readers.

Alan Fowler
Herbertsdale, South Africa

About the authors

Chiku Malunga is the first and leading indigenous wisdom-based organizational development writer. He holds a doctorate in Development Studies from the University of South Africa and is the director of CADECO (Capacity Development Consultants), an organization that promotes African-centred organizational improvement models. With about 20 years of practice, he has wide experience in facilitating organization development interventions with African, American and European organizations.

Charles Banda is an organizational development practitioner working with CADECO. He has many years' experience in facilitating financial and organizational sustainability interventions among non-government organizations.

"Questionable: When many people are ~~include~~ involved, no mistakes will be made

Preface

This book has evolved out of our Organizational Development Awareness Workshops over a period of six years and our practice as organizational development consultants in Capacity Development Consultants (CADECO), based in Blantyre, Malawi. We are grateful to so many organizations that have allowed us to intervene in their lives and to test our developing ideas of using African proverbs in improving organizational performance. To all these people we owe so much. With frequent usage, one's own and other people's ideas sometimes become so intermingled that it becomes difficult to differentiate the two. Special mention and recognition must be made of my colleague Charles Banda, whose level of involvement from the inception of the idea to the completion of the book warrants me to include his name on the cover.

Special thanks go to Rick James for introducing us to the field of organizational development practice and the Impact Alliance. Special thanks go to the Impact Alliance team for their editorial and creative support, critique, and numerous ideas for enhancing the manuscript. We truly appreciate the Alliance's commitment to the project and the patience they have demonstrated. We also thank Meg Kinghorn, Sue Bloom, Evan Bloom, and Christopher Bennett.

Other people have contributed to our development as organizational development consultants. So many writers have influenced our conceptual frameworks. We have deliberately chosen not to include the specific sources of our ideas in the text so as not to disturb the readers' thinking. However, there is a list of our main references at the end. This is by no means a complete bibliography but it shows that we do not claim to be introducing 'strange doctrines'. If we have omitted any other vital sources, we will be happy to be informed. The proverbs in the book have been taken from our own research and from three primary external sources, which you can also find in the References section:

- *The Wisdom of the People* by Joseph Chakanza
- *The Wisdom of Africa* published by the BBC World Service
- *Wisdom of Ancient Times* by Stevenson Kumakanga

It is our sincere belief that, to be truly effective, organizations in Africa and other developing regions must evolve a holistic system of organization that suits their culture and heritage. Direct copying of ideas from Northern or Eastern cultures will not work. We will greatly benefit if we build on the organizational advancements from these areas, but they will only work for us if we contextualize them. When we build this organizational system, the people in the North and East will also benefit by getting insights from us that they can contextualize in their situations. This cross-fertilization of ideas is what is needed for synergy in an environment where the whole world is becoming one global village.

Most authors bring their particular worldviews in their writing. Since no one worldview is entirely right or wrong and in an age where diversity is celebrated, we worry when authors from one worldview dominate the literature on important issues such as organizations. This book is among the first efforts to add diversity to the current dominance of Northern authors on the subject. Further research and documentation will build upon this foundation. It is, however, our modest effort to harness Africa's wisdom in contributing to the collective theory and practice of organizational performance improvement worldwide.

INTRODUCTION
African proverbs as tools for organizational improvement

Rediscovery of the rich and diverse African heritage can make great contributions toward addressing many political, economic, and socio-cultural challenges that the continent and the world faces today. African cultural heritage, passed on from generation to generation, has been a source of guidance for African communities in times of peace, uncertainty, birth, life, and death. It has been the basis of their self-identity, self-respect, and self-confidence. It has enabled them to live in harmony with their physical, social, and spiritual environment.

This heritage provides a foundation for leadership, guidance, problem solving, decision-making, self-reliance, and hope. It helps people to be balanced and focused. Strength drawn from past lessons guides them to the unknown future with confidence.

Rediscovering this under-appreciated and under-utilized heritage and building a society based on the values derived from this richness will enable Africans to find their niche in the world. It will help them address their own challenges more accurately, while strategically positioning them to make a significant contribution to addressing global challenges. This is the essence of African renaissance and the purpose of this book.

This book illustrates how one aspect of African heritage can support this goal. It shows how the traditional wisdom contained in African proverbs can be applied to understanding organizations and improving their effectiveness. The use of African proverbs presents a new and creative way of communicating organizational principles to transcend the common communication barriers.

Interest in collecting African proverbs and using them to enrich modern life is growing, based on a conviction that modern life and institutions would be greatly enhanced if they gave a home to the timeless wisdom these proverbs hold.

This book promotes an understanding of the richness of African proverbs and illustrates how they can be used to understand organizations and help them become more organizationally

http://dx.doi.org/10.3362/9781780447599.001

and financially sustainable. Building capacity for financial and organizational sustainability is one of the most crucial issues facing organizations of all types today. By associating proverbs with organizational issues, the book shows how proverbs can enhance understanding of sustainability issues and consequently how to address them.

More specifically, the book addresses two main themes:

- Effectively communicating financial and organizational sustainability improvement efforts in a language that organizational change leaders immediately and easily understand and in a way that touches their hearts and motivates them to personal and organizational transformation.
- Africa's contribution to organizational theory and practice in a world quickly becoming one global village, where financial and organizational sustainability are key for organizational integrity and impact.

Proverbs and their use

Proverbs are an integral part of African culture. Simple statements with deep meaning, they are guidelines for individual, family, and village behavior, built upon repeated real life experiences and observations over time. Proverbs are mirrors through which people look at themselves – a stage for expressing themselves to others. The way people think and look at the world, their culture, values, behaviors, aspirations, and preoccupations can immediately be understood by looking at their proverbs.

While Africa has many languages, proverbs offer them common ground. The same proverbs recur in similar forms in almost all African languages and societies. Some state facts from people's history, customs, and practices; others express philosophical thoughts, beliefs, and values. Yet proverbs make communication instantly possible, irrespective of differences in geographic origin and cultural backgrounds. Proverbs are the common property of Africans because they are ascribed to the wisdom of all the ancestors. A statement, such as 'so said the ancestors', preceding a saying accords the proverb its unquestionable authority.

According to the BBC's book, *The Wisdom of Africa*, 'proverbs are used to illustrate ideas, reinforce arguments, and deliver messages of inspiration, consolation, celebration, and advice'. More specifically:

- Proverbs identify and dignify a culture. They express the collective wisdom of the people, reflecting their thinking, values, and behaviours. Using proverbs to communicate and understand organizational issues is a powerful tool in the quest for a genuine African identity.
- In traditional Africa, proverbs are used to unlock 'stuckness'; clarify vision, and unify different perspectives. Proverbs add humour and diffuse tension on otherwise sensitive issues. For centuries, African societies have used proverbs to ease uncomfortable situations, confront issues, and build institutions and relationships. They can be understood where literacy is low and yet appreciated by even the most educated.
- Proverbs are metaphors and can explain complex issues in simple statements. For example, two villages in conflict may not fight after reflecting on the proverb, 'When elephants fight, it is the grass that suffers'. The meaning behind the superficial statement about elephants is a powerful message about the negative effects that a disagreement between two chiefs can have on innocent villagers. Similarly, a factional conflict in an organization can be most harmful to those the organization intends to serve – the people in the community. The proverb, 'When spider webs unite, they can tie up a lion': communicates the importance of unity and collaboration in tackling problems and inspires people with the faith that they can address problems together no matter how big.
- Proverbs are like seeds. They only become 'alive' when they are 'sown'. They are simple statements until applied to actual situations, bringing them to life and expanding their meaning.
- As metaphors, proverbs create strong mental pictures. This is a great way to motivate people to action.

Proverbs for communicating organizational issues

While organizational behavior, organizational development (OD), and management principles may be universal, they are not as easy to communicate in many African languages as they are in English, for example. In English, a word like 'strategy' can be used with minimum explanation for it to be immediately understood. But many African languages do not have any direct translation of the word, thus diluting its meaning and increasing the risk of misunderstanding. The power of language cannot be overemphasized. This communication gap may explain why a lot of literature on development and management, mostly written in the North, is without much corresponding translation into action on the ground in the South.

There is no doubt that communication is one of the biggest problems facing agents of change working in organizations and communities worldwide. Only where people are truly communicating is progress possible. Leaders sometimes fail to communicate the organization's vision to staff and other stakeholders in a way that inspires them to transformative action. Consultants sometimes fail to communicate their interventions in a way that ensures lasting implementation and change. Staff sometimes fail to communicate among themselves and with their leaders, leading to conflict and strained relationships. Expatriates and volunteers sometimes get frustrated when they cannot fully communicate with local counterparts and find it difficult to understand some of their values and behaviours.

Ultimately, since proverbs are a vehicle for communication and most organizational problems can be viewed as communication problems, the importance and value of using proverbs as tools for understanding and addressing organizational issues is quite evident.

The audience for this book

This book is about communicating organizational change and improvement in a language people will immediately understand by contextualizing its principles and practices. It will be of particular value to organizational leaders and consultants at all levels wishing to improve the performance of their organizations. Volunteers and expatriates working or coming to work in Africa or other developing countries will learn from the insights into African culture. Students and teachers of organizational and community development or African studies, and development practitioners everywhere will gain from this new use of traditional culture. Donor agencies may find the book particularly appealing as they seek to engage and strengthen their grantees. It will also make good leisure reading for anyone interested in traditional wisdom and how it can be creatively applied to improve organizational performance in particular and modern life in general.

Readers interested in how proverbs can be used to understand organizations may find it useful to read the whole book or simply the chapters of greatest interest. Those interested in improving organizational performance may treat the book as a reflection tool and a guide to specific interventions.

The book forms good material for personal reflection. Organizational leaders and consultants may want to regularly refer to it in gaining perspective on their organizations and practices respectively. Specific assessment tools found at the end of the book can be used or modified for an organizational self-assessment or an individual self-assessment for consultants or leaders. Periodic introspection using the tools will help both leaders and consultants monitor their development and practice.

This book is divided into six chapters:

- The **first chapter** discusses the natural growth phases that every organization goes through as it develops from its beginnings into a mature and sustainable system. It presents the characteristics and challenges facing the organization at each phase.
- The **second chapter** looks at financial and organizational sustainability as a key unresolved issue facing many organizations. It discusses two approaches to financial and organizational sustainability and concludes by showing that the two approaches are complementary but one is more holistic and effective in the long-term.
- The **third chapter** examines the concepts of organizational culture and identity. It presents five types of negative organizational culture and discusses how to create an empowering culture as a basis for organizational and financial sustainability.
- The **fourth chapter** focuses on the importance of leadership in organizational effectiveness and sustainability and ways of developing strong leadership in organizations.
- The **fifth chapter** offers insights on how consultants facilitating change in organizations can improve their own performance so that they can serve organizations better.
- The **sixth** and last chapter argues that organizational assessments are the starting point for organizational improvement efforts.
- The book's **appendix** contains three assessment tools with descriptions of how they can be used. These are the Proverbs Self-Assessment Tool for Organizations, the Self-Reflection Tool for Consultants, and the Self-Reflection Tool for Leaders. The tools are based on the proverbs used in the book.

The reader may notice a seeming shortcoming in the book in that the proverbs may speak louder than our explanations. When proverbs transcend our own experience, the explanation may actually dilute their power. But if a proverb manages to unlock insights from the reader beyond those discussed in the book, this is its strength.

CHAPTER 1
Understanding organizational growth

Organizations are natural social systems that grow and develop over time. This chapter will discuss how to understand the natural growth phases of organizations and the characteristics of each.

Phases of organizational growth

Organizations typically go through three distinct phases as they grow and mature: Pioneer, Independent, and Interdependent.

The Pioneer Phase

Organizations are normally started as the idea of an individual who, with the help of a few friends, implements the idea. Typically, the culture is informal and often run like a family. The pioneer leader acts as a magnet to which everyone is attached. He or she spearheads formation of the organization's identity, vision, values, commitment, and solidarity. The strength of the organization at this phase rests on the charisma of its leader and the power of its values and commitment. These alone are enough to sustain the organization in this stage.

Even the biggest rooster that crows the loudest was once just an egg.

The organization may not have a strategic plan or a clear structure. It might not have a structure at all. There are usually no policies, systems, or procedures. The friends of the leader may not be identified on the basis of their merit but because of friendship

http://dx.doi.org/10.3362/9781780447599.002

or blood ties. At this phase, relationships are usually warm and satisfying. The organization probably does not have a lot of money or resources since it is usually quite small.

This phase is called the 'pioneer' or 'dependent' phase because the existence of the organization is dependent on the pioneer leader. He or she is the source of identity and stability in the organization. Comparing the organization to the life of the rooster, we can say that at this point the organization is still just an 'egg' waiting to hatch. The pioneer organization exhibits youthful characteristics, such as:

- high levels of energy and commitment because the sense of ownership is high;
- personalized relationships and shared tasks among the pioneers (e.g. rotating leadership positions);
- high levels of informality with systems, procedures, and policies being negligible because the group is usually small with high levels of trust;
- verbal communication and rapid consensus;
- shared values and power and high loyalty;
- strong dependence on the leader;
- undefined roles and responsibilities;
- lack of critique;
- learning by imitation;
- naive about reality.

However, like the rooster, the organization cannot remain an egg forever but must grow and develop. The transitions from 'egg' to 'chick' to 'rooster' are often precipitated by crises that cause power shifts in the organization. Crises typically take these forms:

Loss of leadership. The pioneer leader may die, leave, or become incapacitated, creating a vacuum. Without the leader or clear succession plans, people become sheep without a shepherd. This crisis calls for role clarification and differentiation and written guidelines, policies, and procedures.

Growth. Rapid growth in staff may bring new people with different values and beliefs that conflict with the pioneers. Or there may be so much growth that the leader loses control. Newcomers may not share the same values and commitments as the original group, causing confusion as to how things are done and decisions are made. This crisis calls for law and order.

Radical shift in environment. The working environment may change radically, prompting the need to seek a new identity. The crisis may kill the organization. Most of us know organizations that died with their founders. If the transition process is managed successfully, however, it can usher in the second phase of development.

The Independent Phase

This phase arrives as a solution for a crisis in the first phase. Because of the loss of control, plans are made to introduce more order and departmentalization to the system. This phase is characterized by:

- more law and order as policies, procedures, and systems are established;
- more professionalism as clear professional expectations emerge through job descriptions and specialization;
- less personalization as people become known by their titles;
- more fairness as a salary structure may be developed;
- more hierarchy and formality as control is increasingly shifted to the top.

The next natural crisis that shapes the organization is usually a bureaucratic crisis, stimulated by:

- a growing commitment to profession over organization, which hinders the organization as people become more individualistic;
- increased isolation and alienation with less informal interpersonal interactions, failure to identify with the purpose of the organization, separate offices with closed doors, and people known by their titles rather than their names;
- disappearing commitment to values and purpose, leading to boredom and decreased motivation;
- shifting organizational focus to being more self-serving with the needs of the people for which it exists becoming secondary.

This alienation and loss of humanness calls for more flexibility and a better organizational climate. This is done through improving communication, flattening management structures, enhancing team dynamics, managing conflict, and encouraging self-development. These are characteristics of the third phase of organization.

The Interdependent Phase

The third phase is also called the phase of effectiveness because it combines the positive characteristics of phases one and two. Relationships are symbiotic and interdependent in nature. Like extended families, an organization works well only if all of its pieces achieve autonomy. This phase is characterized by:

- individualization changes to a sense of 'we';
- staff drive the organization with a sense of purpose;
- the value base is strengthened;
- the organization is inclusive and effective.

Organizations naturally evolve through these three phases although they may not be as distinct as outlined above. Once the organization has shifted, there is no going back without starting over again. The birth of the new is often accompanied by a crisis. Crisis is an important catalyst for the shift to take place and the organization to break through to a new level of potential. However, a crisis that is not handled well can kill an organization. The key issue is whether an organization chooses to anticipate change and prepare for it or allows change to be forced upon it.

Many of the challenges that organizations face can be better understood through the phases of development. The phase the organization is currently in will also affect the type of interventions that will be most effective. The challenge is to recognize the phase and prepare the organization to consciously move toward the next.

Only in the third phase can organizations become truly financially and organizationally sustainable. Organizational leaders and change agents must create facilitative conditions to speed up the natural processes of the organization to get to this phase of effectiveness and sustainability. Organizations that have not yet reached the interdependent phase should take heart in the knowledge that, as even the loudest roosters were once just eggs, so too the strongest organizations were once in the pioneer phase. Much can and should be learned by nascent organizations from those that have gone before them.

Ubuntu: the spirit of a sustainable organization

While organizations progress through phases in their development, an underlying spirit and strong values must remain a constant in healthy organizations. In Africa, *ubuntu* – the essence of being human –

is a universal value. In traditional African cultures, an individual, family, community, or institution is not primarily judged by external things like material possessions, skills, or competencies, but by the personification of human values. The ideal individual respects himself or herself and others, regardless of who they are. Consequently, the individual, family, and community are all conscious of their responsibilities toward themselves and others. While in traditional African societies *ubuntu* was used to emphasize interdependence in families, we find that it is just as relevant to modern social institutions.

The climax of *ubuntu* is a selfless spirit of living for the betterment of a person's environment using all talents at his or her disposal and not resting easy knowing that another is in need. It is based on the understanding that any good or evil we do to another person or people, we are actually doing to ourselves. This puts us under obligation to support and do good to others. The extended family in Africa is built on this principle.

For organizations to be truly effective and sustainable, they too must be based on *ubuntu* values. They cannot be based just on personality and charisma or on policies, systems, and procedures alone. In its first phase, the values and charisma of the pioneer leader fuel an organization. Often organizations lack adequate resources at this phase. In the second phase, policies, systems, and procedures fuel organizations. While the organization may have adequate resources, those policies, systems, and procedures may stifle the human spirit, making the organization ineffective.

The final phase of development builds upon the informality of the first phase and the organization of the second phase to unleash the human spirit and make human values the fuel for running the organization. This is the phase of effectiveness when practising *ubuntu* values becomes possible. It is toward this phase that all organizations must strive – toward a selfless spirit of living for the betterment of the organization's task environment, using all the endowments at its disposal.

When organizations start calling for values clarification and team-building interventions, it is often because they have lost their *ubuntu* values. If individuals and teams were more conscious of their *ubuntu* values, organizations would be more human and a lot of conflict would be avoided. While more specialization and departmentalization characterize the independent phase, more teamwork and collaboration characterize the interdependent phase. Interdependence, genuine teamwork, and collaboration can only flourish, however, where *ubuntu* values are strong and human potential unleashed, which is the foundation for organizational and financial sustainability.

Growth phases viewed globally

The phenomenon of phases of development can also be observed at the global, continental, national, and community levels. The parallel development at the global level provides a good example to illustrate the three phases of OD. Academics and development practitioners alike increasingly agree that the world is moving into an age of interdependence. It could, therefore, be struggling with how to make the shift from the independent to the interdependent phase. As with organizations, the achievement of interdependence and genuine collaboration must be guided by *ubuntu* values. The North also appears to be struggling with how to make a transition to the interdependent phase as attested by its literature, music, societal problems, movies, etc.

The South on the other hand is generally struggling with how to effectively move from the dependent to independent phase as its literature, music, and societal problems attest. African leaders in the 1960s fought for national and continental independence from colonial powers. Upon gaining independence, most countries on the continent ushered in a dependent, rather than independent phase, signifying a new beginning to the natural process of developing as countries. The charisma and strength of their leaders and strong national values sustained most countries at this phase. For example, while there were no presidential term limits and some leaders could rule for life, people generally did not find any problem with this.

Much of the democracy wave that swept parts of Africa within the last 15 years has been an artificial attempt to move the continent to the independent phase. Those countries that were not ready to shift are caught up 'trying to find their feet' in the confusion of having to live in two worlds – naturally in the dependent phase and artificially in the independent phase. Most of these countries are still struggling with the crisis of the call for formality. This is portrayed by presidents wanting to stay on after their term limits are over, failure to peacefully coexist with people who hold different views, and the general failure of institutions to replace charismatic leaders as the driving force of social development.

A higher consciousness of the phases of development and their implications for development practice is critical for sustainable development. Much of the failure of development efforts in developing countries can be explained by a mismatch between the promoted development efforts and the country's phase of development and the critical issues that need to be addressed. Uncontextualized globalization, for example, may force these countries to jump from dependence to interdependence, which is developmentally impossible. To be effective in such countries, development efforts must aim at laying a strong foundation for political, economic, technological, and socio-cultural independence. It is only after this that effective interdependence can become a reality. In our observation, only in traditional African society can the characteristics of interdependence be observed (e.g. the concept of *ubuntu*). African societies are usually swallowed up and destroyed by their efforts at nation-building, which are struggling in the crisis of prematurely moving from dependent to independent phases, and misdirected development efforts.

This nation-level example of the phases of OD presents two sound recommendations to developing organizations. First, transition through the three phases must happen at the organization's own pace and cannot be forced. Second, and more importantly, the success that traditional African societies had in reaching the phase of interdependence indicates that the wisdom contained in their proverbs may carry particular insights into achieving interdependence.

CHAPTER 2
Strengthening organizational sustainability

The impact the organization makes in its environment, its credibility and accountability to its stakeholders and, most importantly, its financial and organizational sustainability determine the organization's long-term success. Only a sustainable organization can be credible and make lasting impact in its area of work. This chapter looks at how an organization can ensure its sustainability by discussing the two approaches to ensuring organizational and financial sustainability: conventional and OD approaches. The chapter concludes by showing that the two approaches are complementary.

Conventional understanding of organizational sustainability

The conventional understanding of sustainability in organizations focuses on the ability to get money so that activities on the ground can continue. Money is both the emphasis and the target. Means promoted for ensuring sustainability include:

- training individuals in proposal writing;
- diversifying the donor base;
- identifying local sources of money (e.g. social events, dances, big walks, etc.);
- encouraging staff to work as consultants for fees;
- publishing and selling books on experience gained;
- establishing publication subscriptions;
- creating endowment trusts.

Staff members approach people or organizations that have money and convince them to give some money or material resources to the organization. With the ever-increasing number of non-governmental organizations (NGOs), the competition is fierce for getting money for their field of work. In a competitive environment like this one, some NGOs change their focus and undertake other activities strictly for

http://dx.doi.org/10.3362/9781780447599.003

the sake of money, They may be successful only to find that their beneficiaries do not need these new activities now offered.

It is likely to continue to get more difficult to access development funding as increasing amounts of money are being diverted to relief efforts that address global crises. HIV/AIDS, wars, and natural disasters such as floods and droughts take attention away from developmental issues. The old mentality for getting money into the organization may therefore not suffice in this difficult task environment.

Organizational development understanding of sustainability

Recognition comes with having one's own possessions.

Your farm implements are more important than your mother and father.

A borrowed axe doesn't take long to get broken.

In one community, it is told, there was a famous herbalist who could cure almost any disease. His children and relatives were proud of him. They depended upon him to cure them when they got sick and to use the contributions from the other patients he cured to support the family. Although he tried to teach them, no member of the family wanted to learn his skills and secrets. One day he got sick and died. No one could continue his practice since they had not learned from him. They missed his medicine and financial support. They became poor and lived in poverty all their lives.

As in the story above, many organizations are happy to reap the benefits of those around them without putting serious thought into learning how they can get by on their own. In the case of NGOs and community-based organizations (CBOs), this is manifested in their dependence upon external sources of funding, rather than finding ways to make their own money. Learning to build one's capacity to 'cure one's own ailments; or make one's own money is the basis for the OD understanding of sustainability.

With organizational sustainability, though, money is not everything. In one organization, people were voluntarily leaving jobs with salaries in excess of $1000/month (quite high by national standards) to go to organizations where they would earn as little as $50/month. Some resigned simply to stay at home. The reason for these dramatic departures was that despite the high salaries, the staff could not stand the bad relationships in the organization.

The OD understanding of sustainability is more complex and comprehensive than the traditional understanding. OD builds the capacity of the organization to be self-sustaining and attract resources needed to perpetuate its existence, continuously improving its activities with decreasing external support. This means ensuring that an organization properly cares for its proverbial 'farm implements' or human resources and it means putting one's house in order before rushing to look for money from external sources. Without a properly functioning organization to earn the financial resources, money alone is of little value.

At the community level, sustainability means the continuation of benefits after the project has ended. It also means building on the inherent skills and values for sustainability in the community. Communities manage funerals and weddings with their resources, no matter how meager, without external help. Transferring this thinking into community and organizational development is the essence of sustainability.

For example, a group of field officers went to a village where they wanted to launch a development program. In the course of a meeting, they noticed a broken borehole. When they asked the people why they had not repaired it, the people said they were waiting for the government, which had put the borehole there. The officers asked the people if they needed water and if they had any better source in the village than the borehole. The people replied that they indeed needed the borehole and looked forward to the day when it would be repaired. The officers asked the people to contribute on the spot toward the necessary spare parts and collected the equivalent of $200. The needed amount was only $75! The village had raised enough money to repair their borehole and still had some to spare. The lesson from this story is that if development efforts belong to government or an NGO, people will not own them. Where there is no ownership, there is no commitment.

The difference between focusing on getting money into the organization and building the capacity of the organization to generate its own money and to attract other resources is vast. The former looks outward while the latter looks inward. Improving an organization's sustainability from an OD perspective looks at the system in its entirety, starting at the core and moving outward to:

- vision;
- strategy;

- structure, roles, responsibilities, and relationships;
- policies, systems, and procedures;
- skills and competencies;
- resources;
- external relationships;
- culture and values.

The following sections briefly describe some important considerations – also described in African proverbs – for each of those areas.

Vision

Only a tree's necessary branches are maintained while others are pruned and burned.

Just as only a tree's necessary branches are maintained, NGOs are an arm of society and must be relevant if they are to be maintained. Those organizations that are needed by the society (beneficiaries and donors in particular) are supported; those that are not are pruned and burned. To be sustainable, an organization must serve a real and felt need in the society and find a niche that sets it apart from others. When the vision is clear and effectively communicated to the beneficiaries (or created together with them), a sense of ownership and commitment is created.

Many organizations do not take time to communicate their vision to beneficiaries and staff, let alone create it with them. Instead, they go into communities with projects and activities. When people do not see the vision behind the activities and the projects, they cannot be transformed or committed, making it difficult for them to self-organize for sustainability.

Strategy

Money is not everything.

An effective strategic plan enables an organization to understand the minds of those who can give it money. It informs staff how to organize in order to attract needed resources. A strategic plan also enables the organization to look seriously at what resources they already have and how well these are being used. Because of the belief that 'donors will give us money', many organizations greatly under-use the resources they already have. One has just to look at the many government department vehicles that have been parked for minor faults simply because 'a donor will give us another one'. Sustainability means becoming increasingly self-reliant and having a strategy to make the best use of what is available to reduce dependency on external support.

There is a saying that there is no free lunch. If we get a free lunch, it means that someone somewhere has paid on our behalf or we have paid indirectly without knowing it. 'Huge, easy donor money' sometimes tempts organizations. This incredible fortune often comes at a cost. It may mean deviating from our core business or strategy, thereby undermining the impact of the organization and its sustainability.

Structure, roles and responsibilities, and relationships

When cobwebs unite, they can tie up a lion.

An organization that has an effective structure enables the people within it to carry out their roles and responsibilities effectively. Bureaucratic or rigid structures create frustration and inefficiency while flexible structures enhance motivation and efficiency.

To be effective, the structure of the organization must flow from the strategy of the organization. It must also correspond to the development phase of the organization and the context the organization finds itself in. Many organizations, especially small ones, copy or imitate other organizations' structures, especially those of larger organizations. Sometimes they formulate their structures even before they have agreed upon what the organization's work will be and how it will be carried out. Such artificial structures often feel like 'wearing somebody else's shoes that do not fit'. To be effective, structures must be natural and they must also evolve naturally.

Organizational sustainability is possible only when people are working well together. Like the coordinated effort of cobwebs to capture a lion, people within an organization can accomplish much more than they could individually by bringing their various skills together cooperatively. Since the organization's structure determines the roles and responsibilities the individuals and departments carry out (and hence their relationships and interactions in doing so), the structure that an organization adopts becomes a determinant for organizational sustainability. As in the example given above about people leaving an organization because of bad relationships, if staff members leave the organization, it cannot be sustainable.

Because they are busy with project activities, many organizations do not create time to reflect on their structures, roles, and responsibilities and how these are affecting the health of the relationships in the organizations. 'When relationships are bad, most of the energy is spent on internal fights or turf protection and little energy is spent on the realization of the organization's vision, mission, and impact, undermining the organization's sustainability.

Policies, procedures, and systems

Rules are stronger than an individual's power.

There can be no village without rules.

The sustainability of an organization depends on its policies, systems, and procedures and how well they facilitate its work. Donors want to know how their money will be used. While they want to support the people doing the work, they want to see that the major part of the money is going to the community and the people for whom it was meant. Although some donors are unrealistic and ignore the real need for administrative costs, their stance that the money should benefit communities is valid.

Related to this is the role of governance in the organization. For donors, the primary role of the board is its fiduciary role – ensuring that the finances are well cared for as legal custodian of the organization. For that reason, strengthening the board should be a critical part of an NGO's strategy for sustainability. It is unfortunate that many NGO boards are weak and play a minimal role in ensuring financial accountability and transparency. Many boards have been reduced to the role of cheque-signers only.

When NGOs are described as voluntary organizations, this refers to the board. As opposed to the paid staff, board members have no self-interest in the organization's funding because it does not affect their purses. Donors are more comfortable entrusting an NGO with money when they see a strong board, actively involved in raising funds and ensuring accountability.

The key policy area is monitoring and evaluation. Donors want to see their money translating into real change in the lives of the people on the ground. Of late there has been a lot of emphasis on training in monitoring and evaluation and many NGOs now have monitoring and evaluation officers. However, when an organization only does monitoring and evaluation as a donor requirement, it misses the whole point. Monitoring and evaluation must be viewed as a learning process for continuous organizational performance improvement, which is the essence of organizational sustainability.

Skills and competencies

Knowledge is light, ignorance is darkness.

An organization's sustainability is greatly affected by the skills and competencies available and how well these are being used. An organization that has the capacity to write high quality proposals or come up with effective marketing strategies has a better chance of getting donor funds than those that do not. Organizations that are able to attract and retain high quality staff are likewise more sustainable than those that cannot. A strong set of skills and a track record of past achievements provide the organization with a light to find its way forward in even the most challenging of circumstances.

Resources

Prosperity is freedom; poverty is slavery.

Organizations that already have more resources (e.g. reserves in the bank, ownership of buildings, endowment trusts, etc.) and have shown that they are using them well have better chances of attracting resources and being sustainable than those that do not. Success builds upon success. Before looking for more money from external sources, an organization would be wise to ensure that it is using what it already has more productively or to start building upon its resources. As its resources and worth grows, it will become more attractive to external sponsors. When the organization becomes more attractive, it will become easier to raise the extra money needed from external sponsors. Organizations can handle only so much money. The amount of money an organization gets must be matched with the organization's capacity to handle it; the rest is wasted. As the organization both generates and strategically spends additional resources, it gains financial independence and the ability to strengthen its identity as an independently thinking and freely operating organization.

External relationships

One person cannot move a mountain.

No matter how powerful a man, he cannot make rain fall on his farm alone.

Often the difference between where a person is today and where he or she wants to be tomorrow is determined by how well he or she relates to other people. Similarly, the difference between where the organization is today and where its staff wants it to be tomorrow may be determined by how well it relates with its stakeholders. Support and goodwill from stakeholders may play a more crucial role in ensuring the organization's sustainability than its other skills and competencies.

To ensure sustainability, each organization must strategically select the stakeholders with whom it will collaborate. Organizations must seek to add value to any relationship to which they commit and at the same time must make certain that all their relationships are adding and not taking value away. This is the principle of synergy. Any relationship that does not add value is not worth maintaining. This implies that organizations must carefully think through what commitments they will make for networking and collaboration and develop the capacity to say no to those that will not contribute to their effectiveness and sustainability. An organization's success attracts recognition and admirers. While this is good and satisfying, it may also pose dangers. Handling organizational success is as difficult as creating it.

There is a proverb that says, 'Those whom the gods want to make poor, they first send important visitors'. A woman of a successful local community agricultural development initiative had this to say:

When we became successful, we began to receive many visitors. We also got invitations to many national and international conferences. In the process, work suffered. We worked less and less. Recently, I came back from an international conference and found all the pigs dead because there weren't enough experienced people to take care of them.

Organizations must make sure that their successes and the people they attract do not harm their work. Keeping a careful watch over the relationships an organization pursues and nurtures are indeed good for it.

Networking and collaborating only work effectively among mature and strong organizations. A relationship of inequality makes those who are stronger feel that they are 'selling more than they are buying' or that they are being drained by those who are weaker. The implication of this is that the organization must seek those organizations or stakeholders perceived to be strong while building its own capacity to ensure synergy. Stronger organizations may choose to work with weak organizations, but this is a different matter and is usually not partnership in the true sense of the word.

Culture and values

Cutting across all the above factors are the issues of culture and values. While these will be discussed in much greater depth in the next chapter, they bear mention here as a key component of the OD perspective on sustainability. The image and identity the organization creates over time is a major determinant of its sustainability. If the organization is seen as trustworthy, credible. responsive, and professional, it will gain more support from its stakeholders. This means more commitment from both the beneficiaries and the donors, since everyone wants to be associated with a successful organization.

Organizational sustainability is highly context specific. Most of the time answers are found in the most unlikely places. One organization discovered it could make itself sustainable by selling bottled water, since water ran freely from a spring on a farm it owned. CADECO discovered its own mechanism for sustainability when we learned that one of the largest NGOs got 60 percent of its annual operating costs from publications. When we learned this, we began to write.

A key to sustainability is to let people's ideas flow and creatively develop moneymaking ideas. The organization can set up an 'ideas box' in which people can contribute their ideas on how the organization can become financially sustainable. Regular meetings can be conducted in which the ideas are scrutinized for their feasibility and relevance to the mission of the organization. Successful ideas must be implemented and rewarded. It is interesting to note that the most powerful ideas come from the least likely people. Leaders must always be conscious of this.

An organization's leaders, however, must take the initiative to solicit and implement these ideas. Good leaders should know that their organizations might be sitting on a gold mine waiting to be unlocked if only they can open their eyes and see. It is also important to remember that, as a healthy chick comes from a healthy egg, organizational and financial sustainability come from a healthy organization. Creating an innovative culture or building the organization's ability to turn its resources into wealth is the bedrock for organizational effectiveness and sustainability.

Complementarity of the two approaches

If you eat all your harvest, you won't have seed for tomorrow. In your good times, prepare for bad times and in your bad times, prepare for good times.

The conventional and OD understanding of sustainability are complementary. The conventional understanding is concerned with getting money now. The OD understanding is concerned with building the capacity of the organization to get money now, generate its own money in the future, and manage its operations efficiently and effectively. The OD understanding aims at creating an attractive organization rather than persuading donors to give money.

Since we need money both today and tomorrow, organizations must pursue both the conventional and OD approaches. Many organizations get money and relax. They concentrate on project activities and forget the need to build their internal capacity. A weak organization cannot be sustainable. They must be able to get money again. As the harvest proverbs suggest, organizations must be concerned about the present and the future at the same time. It is not enough to have resources for today. An organization must ensure a steady flow of resources into the future, because it is difficult to predict when difficult times will arrive.

CHAPTER 3

Organizational culture as a foundation for sustainability

The primary factor that can enhance or hinder the sustainability of an organization and its benefits is its culture. It is crucial that leaders of change thoroughly understand an organization's culture. Becoming aware of and nurturing the culture of the organization is the first step and the life force of organizational and financial sustainability. This chapter discusses culture as observed in many organizations and explains how to create an empowering organizational culture.

Culture shapes the identity of the organization. The image and identity an organization creates over time is a major determinant of its sustainability. If the organization is seen as trustworthy, credible, responsive, and professional, it will gain more support from its stakeholders. This means more commitment from both the beneficiaries and the donors, since everyone wants to be associated with a successful organization.

What is organizational culture?

The owner of the smell does not notice it.

You cannot tell the quality of the fig fruit by its outside appearance.

Organizational culture is the distinct aroma of an organization. Just as it is difficult to notice one's own odour or that of your house, it is also difficult for people in an organization to be conscious of their culture. Organizations, like humans, are tripartite, made up of body, mind, and spirit. As human beings, we are more conscious of our bodies and minds than our spirits. Organizations are also

http://dx.doi.org/10.3362/9781780447599.004

naturally more conscious of their bodies (financial and material resources) and minds (skills and competencies, policies, systems and procedures, structures, roles, and responsibilities) than their spiritual aspects (vision, leadership, culture, beliefs, attitudes, values, and behaviours). It is this natural tendency to focus on more readily apparent characteristics and to lack a deeper consciousness of one's own inner traits that leads organizations to ignore their cultures.

In more specific terms, organizational culture refers to 'the way we do (or do not do) things around here'. Culture is embedded in the core or inner part of the organization: the values, beliefs, norms, policies, and procedures. It is the informal aspect of the organization that may not be obvious on the surface but that shapes the way people think, behave, and act. Culture is the odour or aroma that an organization produces.

The hidden nature of culture makes it difficult for people to understand and to know whether it is good or bad. On its own, culture is a neutral concept. It becomes good or bad only when it affects an organization positively or negatively. Since culture is unconscious, an organization may not know how it is making the culture work and therefore may not maximize its strength to sustain its success. On the other hand, an organization also may not know how its culture is hindering effectiveness. Its culture becomes the silent killer of the organization.

Just as one cannot tell the quality of a fig by its appearance, many organizations give a good first impression when in reality they are quite different. Outsiders may only look at the glittering objects like the cars, computers, buildings, and personnel in the organization's possession. Outsiders might be surprised to see people leave an organization that seems perfect from the outside. This is because there is often more than meets the eye. Some things cannot be seen but only experienced. Organizational culture is the reality beneath the first impression.

Organizational identity

Because of his double identity, the bat never got a burial.

The person you know during daytime should also be recognizable at night.

The bat has two identities, one as a mouse and one as a bird. When the bat died, the story goes, the birds refused to bury him because

they said he was a mouse. The
mice refused to bury him because
they said he was a bird.

Like bats, organizations often
do not have clear identities or
they have multiple identities.
As culture evolves over time, it gives the organization its identity,
how the organization is perceived by the different stakeholders.
An organization's identity determines stakeholders' expectations.
Organizational effectiveness is achieved when the identity that the
organization wants to create matches the one that stakeholders
have for the organization. Often, however, the identity that the
organization wants to create does not match the one stakeholders
have. Consciously or unconsciously, who we are determines what we
do. If an organization's answer to the question, 'Who are we?' is not
the same as the answer stakeholders give, there will be an identity
crisis with expectations going unmet on both sides.

The importance of a clear, strong identity cannot be overemphasized. When faced with a choice to make among seemingly
similar organizations, people will choose an organization based on
its uniqueness. This uniqueness comes in the form of the identity
that the organization has created in the public's perceptions. Identity
is closely related to lineage and reputation. Pricing difference aside,
when faced with the decision to buy a product or a service, a customer
will choose the organization with the best image and reputation.
Organizations that are not conscious of the image they are portraying
will usually lose out in the long run. Building a strong and clear
identity does not happen accidentally. It is a deliberate effort requiring
consciousness, time, and concentration. It also requires constantly
watching standards and continually improving them.

Many times organizations lose their identity with growth.
The more they grow, the more they lose their cutting edge. These
organizations fail to balance growth with identity or quality. The
identity that they create when they are small becomes a magnet for
more clients. When this happens, they expand and that expansion
becomes their undoing. Organizations must learn to restrain growth
and manage it. Building the capacity to maintain and improve on
the identity and growing in proportion is the best way to manage
growth and ensure long-term organizational success. Just as a person
must remain recognizable during both the day and the night, an

organization should retain a consistent identity throughout its life so as to maintain the trust and relationships that it has built.

Last what is important is not 'who we think we are' but 'who they see us to be'. As exemplified by the proverb about the bat, much of our identity is defined externally. An organization must be aware of how it is being perceived, or 'what they say we are' in order to manage and build its identity. With adequate attention to external perceptions, organizations, unlike the bat, 'will get decent burials', or find acceptance amongst their partners, donors, and peers.

Types of culture

Organizational theorists have classified organizational culture differently. Our practice has identified five main types of negative organizational cultures.

Culture of gossip

When hunting, animals will only come out of hiding when you make a noise.

The man who kicks his old friend for warning him that the path he has chosen is disastrous can only be heading for trouble.

The level and quality of discussion and dialogue in an organization determines the health of the relationships within the organization. These in turn determine how well the organization responds to challenges and opportunities in its task environment, which in turn determines its impact. In many organizations, however, the level and quality of discussion and dialogue is low, leading to inadequate responses and low impact. Such organizations are not able to fully identify the issues facing them and determine how to address them. People in such organizations usually fight symptoms rather than the root causes of the challenges the organization is facing.

Identifying root causes to be addressed requires a lot of 'constructive noise' or input from as many people as possible. It requires people putting their heads together to find a common solution. It requires valuing and respecting all ideas and honestly and transparently scrutinizing them on their feasibility and usefulness. It may involve rewarding people's helpful ideas. As hunting parties can more effectively scare animals out of hiding as a group, organizations can more easily identify their challenges when all staff members work together. When the organization concentrates its energy this way, the 'animals' will come out.

If such capacity is missing in an organization, energy is dissipated. When people sense that they are not given an opportunity to address the issues, or when they perceive decisions are already predetermined no matter what they say, they stop making contributions. They abdicate their responsibilities to those who are mandated to find solutions to the challenges the organization is facing and wait for them to 'screw it up' to celebrate the 'we knew they would fail' attitude.

Instead of spending their time constructively, they spend it on such destructive habits as gossip. People make destructive noise by gossiping among themselves and about the leaders. Through our practice at CADECO, we have observed gossip to be a major poison undermining organizational effectiveness and sustainability efforts. Contrary to popular belief that gossip is a female demon, we have also observed that in fact gossip is a 'gender-balanced demon'.

Gossip is also a major culprit of factionalism and turf wars in organizations. Some have been turned into 'prisons' by gossip. In such situations, people endure rather than enjoy organizational life. They eagerly look forward to the end of the day and weekends to get away from the organization they dread. On Mondays, they think of the ordeals they will have to pass through. In short, people feel better outside rather than inside the organization. In one organization, gossip was so intense that any new staff member was immediately poisoned by departmental colleagues who identified the 'bad guys' in other departments. The prejudices formed and reinforced over the number of years were so intense that the organization got stuck in negative energy, unable to move forward. In this organization, there was noise for sure but it was not directed at getting the animals out. It was aimed at destroying and wearing one another out.

Another form of the culture of gossip is excessive flattery or 'boot-licking'. As a survival technique, individuals who feel inadequate about themselves may use 'boot-licking' to gain favours from those in positions of leadership, feeding leadership with negative information about colleagues. If the leaders tolerate or encourage this, they lose their objectivity and form prejudices against people to their own peril. The leader starts to chase away objective people and surrounds himself or herself with 'yes people'. Some leaders actually plant people in departments to find out what's going on and 'who's on my side and who's not'. This creates an inner circle or 'group-think'. Such behaviors create a suspicious and hostile climate, making it difficult to make the type of noise that will bring the animals out.

Any person who silences constructive negative feedback can only be heading for trouble. A measure of leadership maturity is the ability to handle and cherish negative feedback, to seek feedback from all corners of the organization and to direct staff energy away from destructive and wasteful gossip and 'boot-licking'. Without a conscious effort to do this, organizations risk getting lost down the wrong path and causing irreparable damage. On the other hand, constructive negative feedback brings about awareness of our dark sides. If we work on these dark sides and make enough noise, we can scare out the animals and become more effective individuals and organizations.

Culture of judging people by their appearance

Do not be quick to insult the madman who comes frequently to your doorstep. He may become your mother's husband.

In many organizations, people and visitors are judged by how they look, sometimes before they even speak a word. While looks may portray a certain image, judging people by the way they look develops into a negative organizational culture. As an experiment, we went to a number of organizations, first by driving and the next day by walking. We encountered a warm welcome by the watchman at the gate when we drove. But this same watchman could hardly remember us when we walked. In fact, he gave us quite a tough time getting through the gate.

People must not be judged by how they look, but by the contributions they can make. Looks may be deceptive. People who look important may be useless, and those who look useless may turn out to be helpful. One of our colleagues had a 9:00 a.m. appointment with the director of a company. When he arrived at the reception and asked for the director, the receptionist told him that he could not see the director because he had an important appointment with a Dr Phiri (not his real name). In fact, our colleague was Dr Phiri, but he was also a small man.

Another form of judgement comes when people in higher positions look down and underrate those in lower positions, rarely taking their suggestions seriously. Organizations benefit greatly when they judge people by the quality of their suggestions, rather than their looks or positions. During one intervention we were facilitating in an organization, the tea break started with a set of teacups brought into the room. We noticed that the cups were different. Some were chinaware; others were glass or plastic and one was metal. The first to pick was the director. Her cup was chinaware and contained tea with milk. The last one to pick up his teacup was the watchman. His cup was metal and his tea black. As consultants, we were at a loss as to where we belonged and what cups we should choose. The staff did not seem to find anything strange, but as outsiders, this told us a lot about the culture of the organization.

Culture of secrecy and fear

You cannot hide the smoke when the house is burning.

An antelope cannot drink water when a hunting dog is chasing it.

It is a stupid dog that barks at an elephant.

Most organizations would rather talk about their strengths than their weaknesses. During organizational assessment, some individuals freely express their feelings about the organization and its strengths and weaknesses in private interviews, but do not speak with the same freedom in a group discussing the assessment findings. This is particularly true with issues related to leaders or weaknesses. Sometimes people do not even feel free to speak in the private interviews, despite assurance of non-reprisal. This culture locks individual potential within separate heads where synergy with others cannot be realized. We have witnessed organizations where individuals were punished after a feedback workshop for being too open. In a number of organizations, OD processes were discontinued because the feedback workshop was considered too sensitive. Building an organization means developing strengths and addressing challenges.

The culture of secrecy breeds fear in an organization. People are not free to speak of challenges for fear of punishment or retribution. In our research on factors leading to NGO staff turnover, staff in almost half the organizations interviewed explicitly said, 'We do not want to give you any information because we may be fired'. A number of directors said they could not give out information because the topic was 'too sensitive'. A number said they would get back to us and never did.

When we ask people to name an animal that best represents their organization as they experience it, most come up with potentially harmful animals, such as elephants, snakes, lions, etc. The feeling that their organization is harmful shows that people are fearful of their organizations, especially their leaders. Fear is a major obstacle to releasing organizational potential. People in organizations must be empowered to express what they truly feel and they should be able to talk about both the good and bad sides of the organization. While it is a stupid dog that barks at an elephant, people within organizations must find wise and non-confrontational ways of challenging the status quo.

Some traditional practices reinforce fear in organizations. In one organization in a rural area, we noticed that the director and a few close aides always entered the workshop hall last. When he entered, everyone stood up. In that region, this type of respect was reserved for traditional chiefs. We felt it was not proper behaviour for an organizational leader as it widens the distance between him and the staff. At first we did not know what to do as consultants, whether to stand up with everyone else and show support for the practice or sit down to show protest while everyone else stood. Following the principle of 'start where the people are'; we stood up but took the observation as an opening point to ask the leader in private how he thought the practice affected the organization. On subsequent visits, we noticed that the practice had stopped.

Another manifestation of the culture of fear is when leaders deliberately block the organization's development so that they can remain in control. Such leaders are afraid they will lose control if the organization develops. In such cases, the organization moves to a peak of success. Just as it is about to break through to a new level of potential, the leaders start to frustrate and tear down the promising new leaders to the point that they leave. Then the leaders recruit new staff and 'buy time' inducting them. The organization develops again to a new peak, the leaders frustrate staff again and they leave. The cycle goes on and on, hindering the development of the organization in the process.

In research we conducted among both local and international NGOs in Malawi, 50 percent of the professional staff left their organizations after 18 months. Theoretically, these organizations could have entirely new staffs every three years. Such organizations are not sustainable. They would be more powerful and successful if they could retain their staff. One of the key factors for staff turnover was frustration from the leaders of the organizations. One director said, 'I have been praying that all those who were not supposed to be in this organization should leave. A few have since resigned. I believe God is answering my prayer.' These attitudes often come from fear and insecurity among leaders. It is important that leaders develop themselves as their organizations develop. If the organization develops faster than the leader, he or she may hold back its progress. Ultimately, an organization with a culture of secrecy and fear is much like the antelope that is trying to find nourishment while being chased. The organization's efforts to find sustainability are distracted by fear and uncertainty.

Culture of 'busyness'

When the lion runs and looks back, it's not that he is afraid, rather he is trying to see the distance he has covered.

In the past, time management techniques included both how to manage the time people have to work and free time. Most current time management techniques do not mention how to manage free time because fewer and fewer people have any. We live in a 24-hour society where time has become one of the scarcest resources. There are more and more demands on people's time, leaving them wishing their 24-hour day were extended. This trend has developed a culture of 'busyness' especially in organizations.

In the competitive world, organizations are measured by performance, often tied to meeting project deadlines. This puts a lot of pressure on the people in the organization. As a result, value is given to the doing rather than the being of the organization. There is no time given for learning and reflection. Many organizations, therefore, could learn from the proverbial lion who, despite his power and importance, can still take time to look back at where he has come from. Rather than signifying fear, this reflection provides organizations, like the lion, still greater courage and better preparation for what lies ahead.

In one organization, a consultant was contracted to conduct an organizational assessment. The exercise took a month. Every time the consultant was in the organization, he passed by an open office where a man was sitting in a chair with his legs on the desk apparently asleep. When he completed the exercise and came to deliver the report to the director he said, 'I want to tell you that one of my strongest recommendations is that you fire the man who sits in that office. He just wastes your money and does not work.' The consultant was surprised when the director replied, 'Ah, you mean Simba, that's how he works. When this organization was about to go under, he came up with an idea worth $10 million and saved the organization. He has worked a few miracles apart from that. His work is thinking and producing money-making ideas.'

Creating time and using that time effectively for learning and reflection remains a major challenge in many organizations. Not many organizations have reached a phase of recognizing that reflection and thinking can and indeed should be a legitimate part of work. Many organizations still believe that work means tangible activities. But continuous activities without periodic breaks for reflection and learning are like a refrigerator without a thermostat. They lead to stress, burnout, and exhaustion.

The quality of activities can only be maintained and improved through conscious periodic breaks for reflection and learning. Individuals, teams, and entire organizations must take periodic breaks not only to mechanically review their activities and plan for new ones, but to engage in honest introspection on such questions as:

- What activities are we implementing and why are we implementing them?
- What are our achievements and failures?
- What is working well and what is not?
- What lessons/insights are we drawing from the answers to the above question?
- How can we use these lessons or insights to plan for better implementation of activities?

Most organizations do not believe they have 'enough time' but to ensure long-term effectiveness and sustainability, they must create the needed time. When all that people do on a daily basis is come to the office in the morning, pick bikes, and go to the field, come back in the evening to leave the bikes, go home and hand in a report at the end of the month, interaction and team spirit suffers. Alienation slowly sets in, leading to frustration and meaninglessness.

Reflection periods help people in the organization not only to learn from their activities but also to reconnect with one another and cultivate team spirit. This is why such periods or moments must be spiced with fun, Conducting reflection and learning sessions away from the office, playing games and eating meals together, and, if possible, inviting spouses and families are some of the ways to achieve this. One organization used to spend two days every twelfth week in reflection and learning, called 'back to the nest' days. During these days, all field and office work was suspended and everyone was in the 'nest' reflecting, learning, and having fun.

Each organization must work out what is appropriate within its context. A rule of thumb is that the reflection periods must not be too far apart nor too near each other. When they are too far apart, people may not remember what was learned. When they are too near, the reflection periods cause paralysis.

Under normal circumstances, we do not remember things well because of busyness. If people, organizations, and even countries remembered their experiences, successes, and failures, they would be more successful. This calls for discipline in the way we store our experiences, reflections, insights, and plans, diligently documenting our answers to the reflection questions above. A simple way of doing this is through a 'reflection book'. It may be a simple notebook, a calendar, a daily planner, a diary, or a computer file. A 'reflection book' ensures organizational memory as people leave the organization and new people have a rich heritage upon which to build more success. Such continuity is essential for organizational sustainability.

Another implication of the culture of busyness is that organizations must manage their growth. They must make sure that the amount of work they commit to matches with their capacity to do it. Many times organizations, out of concern for the people they serve or because of 'easy donor money' commit to do work that is beyond their capacity in terms of personnel, skills, and competencies. In trying to meet deadlines in such situations, the people in the organization may hardly have any breathing space. A typical example is the response below from one organization when we asked them to give us permission to interview their staff members for a research project:

> All of us are stressed to the maximum with impossible donor require-ments, which are unrealistic to the technical skills available to a local NGO such as ourselves. We do not have shortage of donors, but we have an overload of highly unrealistic requirements of donor-driven work. For instance, we have 14 donors right now with radically different demands, formats, log frames, financial reporting requirements, and procurement restrictions, We are completely over our heads. We are all exhausted, facing rapid burnout, and your request just comes at a time when I personally can't be respon-sive and none of us in management has an inch of energy left to absorb whatever your findings might be. Anyone of us could resign at any moment based on sheer overload and exhaustion.

Such overzealous commitments fail to recognize that people play multiple roles. For instance, a member of staff might be a husband/wife, father/mother, an employee, a church member, a board member, a student, etc. All these roles require his/her attention and time. A proper balance among these roles is important for effectiveness in life overall, including a job. Organizational demands may prevent them from having balance in their lives or managing the tensions that these roles create.

Culture of fantasy

A bird in hand is worth two in the bush.

Grass may be greener on the other side but it is just as difficult to cut.

A happy man marries the woman he loves; a happier man loves the woman he marries.

Employees tend to think that other organizations are better than their own. This is often more perception than fact. Employees who move to other organizations in hopes of a better life often discover that the gold they sought is not there and cry for their lost paradise. Looking at other organizations as 'greener grass' takes away the spirit and initiative to improve organizations.

With limited employment opportunities, many of us do not find ourselves in jobs we dreamed of when we were young and in school. In one workshop we asked a group of extension workers why they were not as effective as they could be. One of the prominent answers was that 'most of us are in jobs we do not want'. When people come out of school, they are looking for a job and ready to enter any door that may open. There is excitement in getting a job. But once the person starts working, their past usually catches up with them and they start comparing their reality with their fantasy. Consciously or unconsciously, they believe that there are better organizations and jobs out there. Yet perceptions of goodness are usually overrated. This culture is common in organizations that employ many people at the same level, e.g., teachers, extension workers, sales people, police, etc. Leaders must be conscious that they may be leading people who actually regret that they joined that organization.

The feeling of being in an organization by mistake or misfortune forms an infectious mental model that negatively affects the entire organization. This model encourages an inferiority complex as people compare themselves with others. Therefore, teaching people to let go of finding that fantasy job is a major challenge when dealing with this culture. It is important to encourage people to do the best they can where they are and with what they have. They have not 'married the women they loved'. Now they must 'love the women they married'. People must accept that they are not in full control of their environment but they are in control of their lives and the responses they give to what their environment offers. Job satisfaction comes less from the type of work one does and more from a sense of fulfilling a higher mission or purpose. This job may be temporary and a stepping-stone toward whatever one really wants to do in life. An individual giving his or her all to the organization contributes to organizational effectiveness and creates opportunities for advancement in the same organization or in another one.

Another form of this culture is apathy or helplessness. People who grow up in challenging environments and have never seen it get better might develop a negative view of life and believe this view is normal. They stop believing that it is possible to live another and better type of life. They may see others who are living a better life but they believe that those people are somehow special, that they deserve the better life they are living but it is not for them. This worldview can form a culture where people accept the status quo and do not believe in improvement. Their disbelief in the possibility to transform the organization robs them of the energy needed to implement interventions and to reap its benefits. They only experience the self-fulfilled prophecy, 'We knew these things do not work, especially for us'.

This defeatist attitude is much like the envy of the greener grass on the other side of the fence. While we should strive for continuous improvement of our organizations. we must avoid the temptation to live within unrealistic, fantasy visions of our organizations. By accepting our realities, appreciating that a bird in the hand is worth two in the bush and loving the organization to which we are married, we position ourselves to make real progress.

Creating an empowering organizational culture

Only dead people do not speak.

Constructive arguments build a village.

A visitor brings a sharper razor blade.

An outsider sees more in an hour than the hosts in year.

Organizations need empowering cultures in order to find new ways of looking at the world. Empowered cultures enable people to make effective contributions and solicit ideas even from the most unlikely sources. An empowering culture enables people to be transparent and fearless. They take more risks because they do not fear punishment for failure.

However, the most resistant part of any organization is its culture. If it changes at all, the process is usually slow. Culture cannot be changed overnight. The main reason is because insiders become unconscious to the culture and oblivious to odours only outsiders may smell. Negative cultures are self-sustaining and become the shadows that hinder OD. Creating an empowering organizational culture involves bringing the culture to consciousness. Since individuals are submerged in the culture, it may be more effective for an outsider to mirror the organization to them. *Outsiders have a sharper razor blade.*

Another complementary way to create an empowering culture is to encourage a 'culture of talking'. Talking brings life to an organization because only dead people do not speak. Encouraging dissent ensures that when the organization reaches a decision it has been thoroughly looked at from all angles. Many organizations need to develop the capacity for objective discussion and dialogue. We observe meetings where certain people are never given a chance to speak because they always bring out controversial issues. The people we avoid are usually the most constructive and their ideas would transform the organization given a chance.

New employees also see many things initially. A practical point would be to ask any newcomer to write down how they see the organization from various angles (e.g. relationships, policies and procedures, work ethic, etc.) Document and keep these impressions. After a year or two, ask them the same question and document their responses again. Compare the two responses and analyse the results for a picture of the organizational culture.

Yet another way to empower is through reflection and learning and by developing the capacity for conscious self-detachment. Individuals and organizations must be able to observe the organization objectively, concentrating on both the positive and negative aspects. This enables people to see key issues more dearly and to identify what needs to be addressed.

The above processes are meant to bring the shadow to light. The shadow is the dark side, the part we don't know or we try to avoid or hide. We suppress it in the organizational subconscious. When we bring it to the conscious, we can then face it and see the contradictions in our lives and in the organization. Unless we see that there are contradictions in our lives between how we want others to see us and who we truly are, we cannot change. Becoming conscious of this gap is the essence of cultural change and creates an empowering organizational culture. Refusing to face the 'organizational self' is the major factor sustaining negative cultures in most organizations and undermining organizational and financial sustainability efforts.

An organization that continually improves its practice or business will create time and systems for learning. Its people will find meaning in their work and commitment to the organization. An empowering organizational culture creates an innovative spirit. Organizations do not exist for themselves. They exist for the people they serve. Innovation enables the organization to continually self-organize to meet the changing needs of the people it serves. A conscious and empowering culture is the foundation for organizational excellence and sustainability.

CHAPTER 4
Improving leaders' effectiveness

Organizational leaders must consciously manage the culture of the organization to ensure organizational sustainability and therefore its impact, accountability, and credibility. This is the real work of organizational leaders of all levels. This chapter will discuss the importance of leadership in organizational effectiveness. It will also discuss ways of developing leadership effectiveness in an organization.

Leadership and leadership styles

An army of sheep led by a lion would defeat an army of lions led by a sheep.

Life is lived forward but understood backward.

When the beat of the drum changes, so must the step of the dance.

Leadership is the practical application of vision in the organization. Leadership is the life force of the organization. No organization can rise above its leadership and no leadership can rise above its vision. However, a strong leader can draw greatness out of even the least likely places.

There are two complementary concepts of leadership. The first entails actual people holding leadership positions in the organization, such as the board chair and the director. The second concept is that each individual in the organization is a leader in his or her respective roles. The first concept emphasizes direction and the second shared responsibility.

The importance of the direction in leadership cannot be overemphasized. No person can lead anyone further than they have gone themselves. Thus, leaders who have lived through a variety of experiences in their lives can offer their staff the benefit of perspective and understanding by reflecting back on this experience.

However, at the same time, every individual in the organization is responsible for the outcomes of their activities. Organizational effectiveness requires collective effort, calling for shared leadership. Everyone is considered a leader while still respecting the organizational

http://dx.doi.org/10.3362/9781780447599.005

hierarchy. Failure to see every person as a leader or for individuals to see themselves as leaders leads to an abdication of responsibility to only those people holding key leadership positions. Individuals do not feel ownership of the organization or the challenges it faces. Less ownership leads to low commitment to the organization. This encourages a 'them and us' tension between senior leaders and other staff members. An organization that is successful in fostering leadership qualities throughout the organization will gain a degree of flexibility and responsiveness, enabling them to more easily change 'the step of their dance' when the 'drum-beat' changes.

Different leadership styles suit different contexts. Because of the increasing diversity in both people and situations, a particular leadership style may not be effective all the time. Leaders stuck in one leadership style may be effective in one context yet find themselves completely helpless in another. The proverb about changing dance steps with the drum suggests that leaders must respond to each situation and discern the appropriate leadership style. This means that leaders must detach their personality from their style. For example, they should stop thinking that 'I am a democrat' or 'I am an autocrat' because that thinking makes it difficult to make shifts that the environment demands.

Second, leaders must become aware of their natural tendencies and reflect on how these match the demands of the environment they work in. For example, if my natural tendency is toward a democratic style of leadership but I find myself working in an organization of people who are not responsible, I need to shift toward a more autocratic style.

Leaders need to become aware that they usually create comfort zones in their natural tendencies. Making shifts can be difficult and painful. The way to make these shifts is to be 'consciously centred', meaning the leader has to learn how to work with the opposing tensions, such as supporting and confronting, grounding and focusing, giving meaning and energizing.

Supporting and confronting means that a leader needs to move between supporting individuals when they are doing their work well and confronting their behaviours when things are going wrong. People with an autocratic tendency will find it easy to confront while those with a democratic tendency will find it easy to support.

Grounding and focusing means maintaining a balance between learning from the past and creating the future. We have all come across leaders who live so clearly in the future that they ignore current realities and become unrealistic. They come up with huge plans and ideas yet refuse to be subjected to scrutiny, resulting in frustration and disillusion. A person who is always looking at the sky will never discover anything on the ground. Then there are leaders stuck in the problems or glories of yesterday. Given the ever-increasing challenges in the environment, many leaders secretly or openly admire the past and hope it will return. However, the past will not come back. There is nothing we can get from it apart from lessons and insights that can inform today's behaviour in similar situations. Leaders therefore must learn to move like a chameleon – *looking in front and watching behind.*

Giving meaning and energizing means maintaining a balance between making things happen and accepting limitations and working with them, not against. There are so many opportunities and challenges that a leader can turn into stepping-stones both personally and organizationally. But all these require that limitations be accepted. Some leaders see themselves as heroes, wanting to conquer any situation or challenge. In the process, they spend energy that could have been directed more productively elsewhere. Some leaders have a tendency to give up at the slightest opposition. They might miss great opportunities.

Developing leadership effectiveness

Being consciously balanced means knowing what kind of beat is coming from the drums and what type of step is required for the dance. Leadership effectiveness is a measure of how well balanced the leader is. Working on improving one's capacity to be balanced should therefore form a major preoccupation for leaders wishing to improve their effectiveness.

Effective time management

Time never goes back.

Most leaders need to improve their time management. This is a major challenge in Africa. When somebody says, 'I will meet you tomorrow at 2 o'clock African time', that means they will come any time after two. The major explanation is that in traditional Africa there is no value attached to time. There is no difference between 1 o'clock and 4 o'clock as long as there is light. If something is to be done during the day, it will be done as long as there is light. If it is to be done during the night, it will be done as long as there is darkness. This is the rationale for how people treat time in the non-monetary rural Africa. Since this is where most people in Africa come from, its shadow appears in most African employees and professionals.

In Africa, there are only two practical calendars that traditional people value: the agricultural or farm calendar and the human calendar associated with various rites of passage in the human life cycle. These are the only calendars they can directly see reward or punishment if respected or ignored respectively. Calendars based on seconds, minutes, hours, days, weeks, months, and years are alien. A meeting or church service scheduled for one hour may take five hours and people may not complain. African professionals may wear a wristwatch yet find it hard to use as a management tool. Every time management model imported to Africa must take this into account. Leaders must first deal with this shadow in themselves before they deal with it in others.

Modern organizations operate in a different context where time matters. Regardless of whether it is based in Phalombe or Washington, DC, the organization needs to meet targets and international standards. Failure to do so slows productivity. Not dealing with this shadow is one of the major explanations for the failure of organizations in Africa that have done well elsewhere. Since time never goes back, the challenge in this context is clearly how to help employees and professionals deal with this shadow and to help rural people see value in managing time well.

Concentration and focus

At the crossroads, you cannot go in both directions at the same time.

He who cannot rest cannot work; he who cannot let go cannot hold on; and he who cannot find footing cannot go forward.

He who does not know where he is going will never know when he has arrived.

One of the ways to improve leadership effectiveness is to develop the capacity to concentrate only on those activities that are critical Doing more often means achieving less. Many leaders are caught up in too many activities and too many roles both inside and outside the organization. Rising on the social ladder means the number of demands on time also rises. To be effective, leaders must develop the capacity to be realistic and say no to what may distract them from more important things. At the proverbial crossroads, leaders cannot and should not try to go in both directions, as they will end up going nowhere.

We have seen organizations where the leader is rarely found in the office because he or she continuously moves from one meeting to another. They come back to the organization only to leave for a workshop that others, even juniors, could attend and bring back benefit. Organizational effectiveness requires that the leaders be present in the organization and that they concentrate only on those activities that will make the best use of their time, experience, and skills. Leaders must spend time at the office and delegate trips as much as possible.

Besides focusing one's current efforts, another important aspect of leadership is keeping focused on the overall direction of the organization. Too often, instead of being forward-looking, leaders look downward. They focus on activities and forget the vision. Failure to focus on the vision or destination may cause an organization to go astray from its intended path, or to lose sight of its progress. Continuous reflection and understanding of the vision generates 'leverage' activities, or those with the least number of tasks that will render the greatest impact. Improving leadership effectiveness means taking regular periods of time to reflect on the activities one engages in and the contribution they make to personal and organizational effectiveness. What is no longer necessary is pruned and burned.

Leaders can use exercises to improve their focus and concentration skills. At first, they will seem difficult. With practice, however, practitioners gain more and more control and the ability to concentrate and focus. This requires patience.

If a leader approaches self-development with impatience, he or she will destroy it. Some of these exercises include:

Concentrating thoughts. For five minutes every day, focus on a simple object that in itself has no interest for you. This exercise is the simplest to talk about but the most difficult to do. Describe the thing to yourself in great detail, or imagine the process that went into manufacturing it without deviating. Initially, your thoughts are inclined to go somewhere else, which shows how we are not free in our thinking.

Juggling. Juggling builds the capacity for concentration and the ability to maintain a rhythm for handling multiple tasks.

Balancing. Balancing a stick on a finger builds the capacity for concentration and focus for doing one thing at a time without being distracted. In traditional Africa, young girls are taught to balance a clay pot full of water on their heads and walk from the well to their homes without holding it with their hands for this reason.

Daily reviewing. Look back; review your day just before you go to sleep. Think backward from the last thing you have done to the first thing in the day. Picture in your mind what you were experiencing, hearing, feeling etc. The ability to reconstruct the day without deviating builds the capacity for concentration and seeing things through.

Strengthening resolve. Decide that the following day at a specific time you will perform an action that has no specific purpose whatsoever. You will forget to do it time after time until your capacity to act with resolve is strengthened. This exercise demonstrates that we are masters of our own lives, but we are less in control than we would like to think.

Being approachable

The path to the chief's house does not grow grass.

Because leaders travel frequently they often find that work has piled up when they return. In trying to catch up, they may not have the time to be available to their people. Some leaders believe in maintaining their power by being a myth and therefore not available to their people. To be effective, however, a leader must be approachable and available to the people he or she is leading.

Leaders must create time when their work will be listening to and talking with the people they are leading. They must have an open door policy. In addition to walking to people's offices, they must let people walk into their offices freely. 'The path to the chief's house does not grow grass' because people are always trampling on it as they are going there.

Teach by example

A crab's daughters cannot walk differently from their mother.

Character is like pregnancy; you cannot hide it for long.

The mother crab had two beautiful daughters she hoped would both marry princes. Her only worry was that she did not like the way they walked, which was sideways. One day she called them and said, 'I am going to teach you how you should walk. I will teach you how to walk straight. If you want to walk straight, you should walk like this.' She demonstrated how to walk and asked her daughters to walk like she had, which they did. They walked sideways!

Leaders in organizations set standards not necessarily by words but by actions. Leaders cannot say one thing and do another and then expect people to follow what they say. Their words and actions must match. Integrity is a major component of leadership effectiveness. Leaders must teach by example, act as role models, and personify the organization's values.

People must be able to see the organization and what it stands for in the leaders' lives. When leaders are divided against themselves, they reduce their own power. They cannot punish somebody coming to work late when they themselves come to work late without guilt. Effective leaders resolve any conscious contradictions in their lives and seek feedback to do so. Then they will speak with authority and command the respect of others. Like the mother crab, leaders lead best through example and must be prepared to 'walk their talk' if they expect their staff to follow them.

Widening personal and organizational exposure

To one who has never travelled, a small garden is a big forest.

The eyes that have seen an ocean cannot be satisfied with a mere lagoon.

You can only jump over a ditch if you have seen it from afar.

Organizational vision is limited by the exposure of its leaders. The challenging environments present in most of Africa constrain organizational vision. When people see mostly problems and hardships, imagining a life of solutions can be quite difficult. During a national vision-crafting consultation in communities, people kept talking about what problems they would want to eliminate, rather than the changes or solutions they wanted to see.

Leaders must transcend their current constraining environments and situations by widening their exposure. Conflict will arise if members of the staff have more exposure than the leader. Since no organization can rise above its leadership, leaders create the ceiling. Individuals more exposed will feel that the leaders are blocking their growth and development. Leaders must have the strongest telescopes and widest horizons in the organization in order to see the farthest and widest. Strategies for doing this include making use of modern facilities like the internet, reading, attending international seminars, and joining professional clubs.

The responsibility for increasing personal exposure extends to encouraging staff members to go beyond their familiar environments. A leader must encourage staff to appreciate the larger world outside the organization, a world of opportunities from which they can reap for the benefit of the whole organization. Some ways to do this include establishing peer partnerships, modelling an admired organization, and encouraging exchange visits and placements, self-development programs with groups from diverse backgrounds, and membership in professional clubs.

Great leaders bring critical perspective to an organization. They enable staff to understand the challenges they face, to think beyond a limited world view, and to truly grasp the possibilities that lie before them.

Leadership succession

When a reed dries up another one grows in its place.

A true measure of a leader's success is the health and strength of the organization he or she leaves behind. Organizations normally live longer than any one individual, meaning that a leader will normally be replaced at some point. Therefore, for the sake of organizational sustainability and continuity, leaders must carefully plan for their succession. Many organizations, especially those in their pioneer phase, die with their leaders for lack of such a plan.

We have worked with development organizations started by individuals who give the impression that this is their organization and they cannot give it to anyone else. This attitude is detrimental to the effectiveness of both the organization and its leadership. Leaders must realistically and periodically assess their work to see if they are still making a significant contribution. When this is no longer the case, they should move on and make room for others.

Chieftainship in Africa is hereditary, which implies that becoming a chief is for life. Unfortunately, this is the model leadership with the most exposure. When people become leaders in organizations and government institutions, consciously or unconsciously they tend to want to adopt this type of leadership. As a result, they do not have succession plans. This explains the phenomenon of life presidents, life directors, and life board members, for example. Since succession is hereditary, the leaders may feel more comfortable handing the mantle to a relative or a dose friend. This friend or relative, however, may not have the same leadership ability or the handover may violate the organization's bylaws and principles.

One observation we have made is that some leaders know they are not able to work any more miracles but hang on because they do not have anything else to do. A major way of improving effectiveness is for a leader to plan for his or her own life after leaving the organization well in advance. This allows for more objectivity in decision-making and reduces the need to defend a position at the expense of the organization. Awareness of this limited duration will also ensure a smooth transition for the next leader and give him or her a stronger heritage to build upon.

The same also applies to boards. We have met board members who have been present since the beginning, some for twenty years. Such people usually hold the organization in the past. One participant in a workshop voiced his challenge, 'If we say that democratic presidents cannot stay in office for more than two terms, should directors and board members in public organizations be allowed to stay?' No one is indispensable, hence the saying 'When a reed dries up another grows in its place'.

Leaders must, as much as possible, try to develop their successors from within rather than getting outsiders. While getting an outsider may bring a 'sharper razor blade', in most cases, the disadvantages outweigh the advantages. Bringing in outsiders before first looking within the organization may bring frustration, resentment and low self-esteem among the potential leaders within the organization.

In order to ensure effective leadership and therefore its sustainability, it is important that an organization address from its formation the issues of how it is going to develop its leaders and how the transition from one leader to the next will be handled. For organizations in the pioneering phase, the sustainability of the organization is closely tied to the leader or leaders. These leaders however must have the wisdom to know when to bow out. For organizations that have moved to the second or third phases, it is important to set term limits for tenure of key leadership positions like the director and board members and ensure that these limits are being adhered to.

Beginning with their recruitment interviews the leaders must be asked to start thinking about their life after the organization. In most cases, the organization must encourage and support the individuals in their plans. One way of doing this is to encourage the leaders to undergo self-development processes, a key component of which is to come up with a personal vision of how they see themselves in the future and the steps they will undertake to make the vision a reality. Most organizations have a vision and strategic plan but the leaders within these same organizations often do not have personal visions and strategic plans.

A clear personal vision and strategic plan lessens one's fear of the unknown future and helps the individual to be more in control of his or her life. As his or her time is coming to an end, the leader must cultivate potential leaders from within the organization and consciously start delegating more and more responsibility while slowly withdrawing from the central role, which helps to ensure a smooth transition. We have observed that in some organizations, when directors move out of their positions, they immediately move to the board, often taking the position of chairperson. Such arrangements usually make it difficult for their successors to establish themselves. Former directors may also be tempted to meddle. It is usually better for former directors to leave their organizations completely. They may act as advisors but they should not have any direct role. They may also serve on the board after some time, say a year or two. By this time, new directors should have established themselves and the likelihood of meddling is low.

CHAPTER 5
Improving consultants' effectiveness

Organizational leaders and consultants work together in cultivating organizational sustainability. While the primary role of organizational leaders is to find solutions to their organizations' challenges and demands, the primary role of consultants is to help the leaders better understand the challenges and demands so that they can find more effective solutions. This chapter discusses some lessons for organizational consultants and provides insights for improving their effectiveness as organizational change agents. This chapter is also important because it is a guide for organizational leaders to recognize effective consultants.

Role of the consultant

The process by which an organization matures through the pioneer, independent, and interdependent phases and to its ideal picture, is a natural one and can happen in a number of ways. The role of the consultant as change agent is to facilitate and bring more consciousness to the process. One of the ways is through OD. OD is a holistic approach to improving an organization's impact, sustainability, and integrity, aimed at creating and nurturing an empowering organizational culture as a basis for organizational improvement efforts. According to French and Bell:

> OD is a long term effort, led and supported by top management, to improve an organization's visioning, empowerment, learning and problem solving processes, through an ongoing, collaborative management of organization culture with special emphasis on the culture of intact work teams and team configurations, utilising the consultant-facilitator role ... (1995: 28)

Since different kinds of interventions might be employed in improving organizational effectiveness, some of the signs indicating that OD would be more appropriate are:

- The same problem keeps recurring despite various efforts to arrest it.

http://dx.doi.org/10.3362/9781780447599.006

- There is a problem in the organization but no one can figure out exactly what it is.
- The organization is faced with dilemmas too difficult to resolve.
- The organization is contemplating or has experienced major changes (e.g. changes in size, focus, identity, strategy, and/or projects).
- There is confusion about identity, roles, and responsibilities.
- There are high levels of staff turnover and frustration.
- There are relationship problems; individuals, departments, board and staff disagree. The high levels of suspicion and lack of trust cause people to be happier outside the organization than inside.
- Departments or projects become too autonomous, creating coordination problems.
- There is a general lack of commitment to the organization and its goals.
- People feel powerless and energy is spent on pointing fingers at each other rather than addressing problems.

In short, the OD process is appropriate for organizations that are:

- in a crisis;
- doing well but facing a crisis in the short or long run;
- doing well but wishing to build on their strengths for even more success.

In working with the client organization, organizational consultants play different roles as the situation demands. Each situation is unique, requiring a unique response. The main roles organizational consultants can play are:

Supporter. The consultant gives the client organization a sense of worth, value, acceptance, and support in its development efforts.

Raiser of consciousness. The consultant helps the client organization generate data and information in order to restructure perceptions. The consultant acts as a mirror of the reality of the situation and how things could be.

Confronter. The consultant points to value discrepancies in the beliefs and actions of those working in and with the organization.

Prescriber. On rare occasions, it becomes necessary to tell the client organization what to do to solve the problem.

Trainer. The consultant teaches the client organization concepts, frameworks, and principles so that the client organization can diagnose and solve its own problems.

MAJOR TYPES OF OD INTERVENTION	
DIAGNOSIS	To ascertain problems. Traditional data-collection and fact-finding methods are commonly used, including interviews and questionnaires
TEAM BUILDING	To enhance the effective operation of systems
INTER-GROUP	To improve the effectiveness of independent groups. The focus is on joint activities
SURVEY FEEDBACK	To analyse the data produced by a survey and design appropriate action plans based on collected data
EDUCATION AND TRAINING	To improve skills, abilities, and knowledge of individuals in areas such as leadership and governance development and financial management
RESTRUCTURING	To improve the effectiveness of the technical or structural aspects affecting individuals or groups. Examples include job enrichment, matrix structures, and management by objective
PROCESS CONSULTATION	To help managers understand and act on human processes in the organization, such as leadership, cooperation, and conflict, managing organizational culture; formulating policies, systems, and procedures development
GRID ORGANIZATION DEVELOPMENT	To use a six-phase change model involving the entire organization
THIRD-PARTY PEACE MAKING	To manage conflict between two parties
COACHING AND COUNSELLING	To better enable individuals to define learning goals, reflect on how others see their behaviour, explore alternative behaviours, and learn new ones
LIFE AND CAREER PLANNING	To help individuals identify life and career objectives, capabilities, strengths and deficiencies, and strategies for achieving objectives
PLANNING AND GOAL SETTING	To include theory and experience in planning and goal setting. May be conducted at individual, group, or organizational levels
STRATEGIC MANAGEMENT	To help key policy makers identify their organization's basic mission and goals; ascertain environmental demands, threats, and opportunities; and engage in long-range action planning

Source: adapted from French and Bell, 1995

OD consultants can perform these roles in a variety of different types of interventions. These interventions correspond roughly to the types of challenges that an organization may be facing, from weak leadership or interpersonal conflict to restructuring and strategic planning. These interventions can be grouped into 13 types. By understanding which type of OD intervention he or she is working in, an OD consultant will be better able to focus his or her energy, as well as the energy of the staff of the organization.

Lessons for consultants

The following are some of the lessons consultants can use to improve their effectiveness.

Need for personal transformation

A changed place cannot transform an individual but a transformed individual can change a place.

Intervening in the lives of other people and organizations is an enormous responsibility with serious implications for the consultant. The essence of organizational change interventions is transformation. To bring about sustainable change in the individual or the organization, change must occur on a deep level or start at the core of the organization. It is a simple human principle that people cannot give what they do not have. Consultants cannot bring about individual, team, and organizational transformation if they are not transformed themselves.

Good consultants are alive and awake all the time. They involve their whole being in each undertaking. They stay in touch with their purpose and use their skills, experiences, emotions, and position rather than being used by them. They go with the flow but are not afraid to go against the majority. They live in different worlds without being swallowed by any. They see dilemmas as opportunities for creativity. They see the environment through the eyes of purpose. Therefore, in order to be effective, organizational practitioners must not neglect their own self-development.

Another aspect of the above proverb on transformation points toward the need for people in the organization to change for the organization itself to change. The work of organizational consultants must ultimately be directed at transforming people and not merely things. Even the best structures, strategies, and systems sooner or later reflect the heart of the people in the organization. On the other hand, transformed people clearly see the need to change and improve even the worst structure, strategy and systems.

While changing things and people usually go together, focusing on transforming people is more important because this is where the sustainability of change lies. Transformed people can change things themselves and because of this they will own and sustain the change.

Marketing consultancy services

Good merchandise sells itself. If someone offers to cover you in cloth, you should first see what clothes they are wearing themselves.

Organizational improvement practice in NGOs, especially in Africa and other developing regions, is still new. As such, awareness of it is also low. The concept of capacity-building among many NGOs remains limited to the acquisition of material resources and training. The full benefits of process interventions are still not known. For this reason it is important for organizational consultants to think through how they will market their services.

One of the major lessons we have learned from CADECO's practice is that aggressive methods do not work when it comes to selling organizational improvement services. As long as people do not feel any pain in their organizations, they see no need for calling for a consultant. In fact, leaders are often reluctant to call in consultants because they cannot differentiate between what situations can be better handled within the organization and what situations call for external consultants.

Organizational leaders will often call for consultants only when they:

- have been told by donors to carry out an evaluation or a baseline survey and they dare not disobey their donors;
- have a deep problem threatening their survival or that of the organization.

In other words, leaders generally call organizational improvement consultants only in limited situations. The long-term nature of process interventions explains why few go through a complete organizational change program. Once the pain that motivated them to call for help goes away after the first or second intervention, they discontinue the process to the detriment of the organization.

The marketing implications of this are that, like a medical doctor, the consultant cannot force an organization that does not feel pain to come to the clinic. Directly soliciting work backfires in most instances since it gives the wrong signals to the potential client and reduces the power of the consultant.

A more effective way of marketing organizational improvement services is to make one's service and one's self more attractive to potential clients. More effective ways of marketing organizational improvement services involve bringing awareness of process consulting, its benefits, and how it works to potential clients. If possible, give concrete examples of similar organizations that have greatly benefited from similar services. The aim is to make potential clients:

- know you and the uniqueness of your services;
- trust you, your knowledge and experience: 'Show the clothes you are wearing';
- prefer you to your competitors;
- choose you rather than your competitors.

Overall, the strongest marketing strategy for the organizational consultant is to provide high quality service.

Listening to everyone

Taking action based on one person's view is provoking wasps in a nest.

Consultants must be conscious of special dynamics. Often clients will come to the consultant with a predetermined problem and preconceived solution framed from the point of view of a small number of people in the organization, usually the leaders. For example, a client may come and ask the consultant to help stop the problem of high staff turnover. In order to truly help, the consultant must not rush to prescribe solutions before fully understanding the problem and its underlying causes. He or she needs to listen objectively to all parties in the organization.

It is important to maintain the attitude that everyone has something worthwhile to say no matter who they are. There is always a danger of the consultant being swayed by more persuasive individuals in the organization and ending up siding with one particular group only to earn resentment from another. Because some people are not able to speak freely in workshops or group settings, it is important to carry out anonymous individual interviews so that those people can freely speak their mind.

Since the leaders often frame problems, it is important to prepare them for any surprises that may come from the interviews. Often those in leadership see things differently than the staff does, which often causes the problem. Leaders tend to disassociate themselves from problems because they are the ones asking for the consultant's help and often work closely with him or her. This gives them the impression that they are part of the solution rather than the problem and that the problems lie with other members of the organization. On the other hand, other members might think that the leader is the problem and removing him or her would do away with all the problems.

Seeing beyond words

To see a snail's eyes, one must be very patient.

To the man who has only a hammer in his tool kit, every problem looks like a nail.

Each person and organization has a shadow that they try to protect. We all tend to think that we are good people and that if there is a problem, the other person must be to blame and not us. When talking to people therefore, the consultant may not be able to get the full picture of the problem from words alone. A full range of skills and tools is critical for a consultant to be able to effectively address the wide range of OD needs he or she will encounter. In particular, the consultant must develop skills to see beyond the words and see hints in the way people interact, the way offices are arranged, the artefacts in the building, such as wall hangings, the way resources are allocated and utilized, etc. He or she must be able to observe these and bring contradictions to the consciousness of the individuals and groups concerned. This is a critical skill for helping organizations to move beyond their stuck points.

We once found a hanging on a director's wall that read, 'It is better to work alone than work with fools'. Most staff members said they believed the hanging reflected the director's true thoughts more than the team spirit he encouraged in the organization. The director may have put the hanging on the wall innocently and with the good intentions of encouraging others to be wise. However, the words on the hanging may have been a true but unconscious reflection of his lack of trust in the wisdom of the staff.

For the consultant, seeing what the leaders of the organization are not seeing is a key skill in helping organizations move from their stuck places. Sometimes this demands a great deal of patience, but ultimately, people can only transform when confronted with the contradiction of what they say they are and what they truly are.

The quality of questions

It is the hand that tied the lion that knows best how to untie it.

One type of intervention, process consulting, bears special attention. (See the table earlier in this chapter for a list of the major types of interventions.) The key difference between a process consultant and other consultants is that the process consultants bring questions to organizations rather than providing solutions. The basic belief in process consulting is that solutions people create for themselves are more relevant and long-lasting than those coming from the outside. The key to creating these solutions is through working with developmental questions. Solutions are situation-specific; what worked in one organization may not work in every organization. No one knows their situation better than the leaders of the organization do. Developmental questions are the means to surface situation-specific solutions. While providing guidance, the consultant asks questions that help staff to:

- focus on the issues at hand;
- observe trends, patterns, and events that will help explain the issue;
- dig deep to understand the underlying causes of the problem;
- state what they want to see changed in the situation;
- evaluate alternative actions to be taken, based on their consequences;
- analyse obstacles to be overcome;
- identify what can be done from within the system and what external support is needed;
- decide upon the best action and how it will be taken.

The answers to all these questions can only be found within the organization because, at some level, those inside the organization know best how the organization operates and what is needed to strengthen it. The consultant only encourages the organization to open its own bag of solutions.

Process consultancy success greatly depends on the ability of the consultant to ask the questions the client would ask. The questions must express his or her understanding and interpretation of the client's own, real questions concerning the situation or issue at hand. The consultant also must support the client to live with the question or questions without rushing for immediate answers. The more the client holds the question, the more it grows and the more it awakens consciousness within the client's system. It is important, therefore, that the consultant listens deeply so that he or she can express the real question(s) of the client and not his or her own. While the consultant may find the words, he or she must always ensure that the question, and eventually the answer, comes from the client.

Intervening into organizational culture

A guest sees more in an hour than a host does in a year.

A finger does not point at its owner.

Culture has a tendency to sedate all who come into it. Remaining conscious takes effort. The influence of culture takes over so gradually that it usually is not noticed. New people see so much in a new setting that gradually fades with increased exposure.

The greatest leverage the consultant has is that he or she is an outsider to the client system and is able to see far more than the people inside the organization. The lesson for consultants is that in order to effectively help the organization, they must always maintain newness and avoid being swallowed up by the culture of the organization. Consultants who have been absorbed by the culture of the client organization stop being objective and effective. Working in an organization as a consultant for a long period of time can be dangerous. It is better to work for short periods of time with breaks rather than establishing a permanent office in the client's organization. This is a particular challenge for organizations' internal consultants.

Another advantage consultants have is to be able to 'speak the unspeakable' because they are not caught up in organizational politics. People in the organization often do not give each other adequate feedback for fear of destroying relationships. The proverb about the finger is particularly true in this respect as staff members are usually reluctant to implicate themselves or their close colleagues as contributing to problems within the organization. But, sometimes admitting to being part of the cause is the first step to finding a solution. A consultant is above these fears and is capable of giving the constructive feedback that could be the most effective way of helping the organization move from the places where it is stuck.

Intervening into power and organizational politics

One cannot tell who is going to lose until the fight is over.

While coming from a walk with his children, the little frog was confronted by a francolin[1] and they started to fight. Terrified by the gigantic size of the francolin as compared to their father, the frog's children ran home and told everyone that their father had been killed. When friends and family members went to the site of the fight to collect the corpse of the frog, they were surprised to see the frog alive and the francolin dead. While the francolin was physically stronger, the frog had a poisonous skin that killed his opponent. The moral of the story is: do not judge who will die before the fight is over.

When consultants go into organizations, they must be aware that they are intervening in a political system where different types of power interplay. They must be able to identify the power points and how these affect organizational effectiveness. The picture of power on the surface may not be the real one in practice. There are organizations where a secretary wields more power than the director, for example.

Power is connected to decision-making. In the wrong hands, power leads to negative politics. Powerless people cannot make big decisions. The role of the organizational practitioner is to help organizations establish positive politics. This is one of the most complex roles an organizational consultant plays and it calls for a lot of maturity. The consultant must analyse the power politics of the organization, identify the positive and negative elements, and then intervene to strengthen the positive elements and diffuse the negative ones.

No one wants to be stripped of power and individuals naturally resist any efforts perceived as doing so. Consultants must know how to deal with resistance in individuals, groups, and organizations. Power dynamics often become clear in conflict management and resolution interventions. Power translates into the ability to do work. Therefore, identify people with power, either positive or negative, and work with and through them to be effective.

Coaching and accompaniment

What elders see while sitting, the young may not see while standing on their toes.

No matter how sharp a knife, it cannot cut itself.

It was ignorance that made the rat challenge the cat to a wrestling contest.

Organizational consultants must be realistic about their capabilities and be able to measure their capacity against the interventions they are being asked to undertake. It is important to recognize one's limitations and work with and not against them. Consultants must not attempt to climb trees that are too high for them. This is why the process of self-development is of such critical importance in the organizational consultant's life. Frequently, young, inexperienced, and overzealous consultants undertake assignments bigger than their capability. Such consultants must be reminded of the rat wrestling the cat. These consultants may do more harm than good and the organization's staff usually ends up frustrated and confused. The importance of thorough knowledge and experience cannot be overemphasized.

It is important for young consultants to have older and more experienced consultants as coaches and mentors. A mentor is someone who has succeeded in a professional field and is prepared to help a less experienced person grow. A mentor provides guidance and advice in such areas as getting started, providing services more effectively, filling a specific niche in the market, and promoting services. A coach provides specific assistance with specific problems. A coach may teach clients how to improve negotiation or communication skills to make better deals when contracting with a client.

When faced with a new intervention, it is important to work under a more experienced consultant and learn from him or her. Having a coach and mentor is one way of hastening self-development. Consultants also need speaking partners with whom to regularly exchange ideas and gain different perspectives. We all have tendencies that are helpful in some situations but not in others. Speaking partners enable us to see where our natural tendencies may not work or where they go off on a tangent.

Empathizing with the client

The sympathizer cannot mourn more than the bereaved.

Consultants must remember that the problems of their client organizations are not their own. The consultant's role is to help people, not carry their problems for them. Many times people tend to throw the problems on the consultant. He or she can empathize but taking problems on as his own is wrong. Indeed, if consultants took on the problems of all their clients, the amount of stress would be indescribable. Consultants must have faith that people have the capacity to deal with their own problems; limitations only come from inadequate and inappropriate knowledge and information. The role of the consultant, therefore, is to provide the information, knowledge, and alternatives necessary for the client to make informed choices. The consultant has no power to change an organization; only the people in the organization can, if they choose, and at the pace that they choose as well.

When faced with a desperate organizational situation, the temptation is high to become too sympathetic and the line between sympathy and empathy becomes blurred, leaving the consultant open to losing objectivity. Lasting solutions to organizational problems are the ones that people create for themselves. It is difficult to facilitate this process when the consultant is too sympathetic and encourages dependence, taking away the client's sense of responsibility. Going through a process intervention is like going through treatment for tuberculosis where the symptoms disappear within a few days of starting medication. To be fully cured, the patient must go through the whole prescription, which may take up to a year. If the patient stops taking the medicine, the disease may come back even stronger. And because it did not truly go away in the first place, it is more difficult to treat the second time.

The same is observed in many organizations. After the first in a series of interventions is conducted, the pain usually disappears. People may not feel the need to continue, frustrating the efforts of the consultant to follow up and sustain the process. Draft reports may not be read and attempts to follow up may be met with indifference.

While consultants are usually motivated by their passion for the practice and their desire to see the process through to the end, they must remember that they can only go as far as they are allowed. They cannot mourn more than the bereaved. The consultant may take solace in the thought that the organization is only postponing the problem. It will return and so may their work together.

Ensuring ownership of interventions

You can take the goat to the river, but you cannot force it to drink the water.

Three issues critical for a consultant to consider before starting the process as preconditions for sustainability are readiness, time, and other resources. The leadership of the organization must be genuinely committed. The staff must take more ownership of the process than the donors. The time needed for the process must be agreed upon in advance. The time frame depends on the scope of the change and depth of the intervention. For large organizations, the process may take anywhere between 12 to 24 months on a cycle of two to five years. It is also important to agree on and commit to the overall resources needed for the process, including staff time, meetings and workshops, consultants' fees, etc.

The true success of any organizational intervention is how well the intervention is implemented after the consultant has left, implying that change has taken place within the organization's culture. When an intervention is over and the consultant gone, the staff has to decide whether it will use the strategic plan as a management tool or merely as a means for getting donor funding. It decides whether to sustain the team spirit developed during team building sessions or let it die. Only the staff can decide to use the policies, systems, and procedures developed. Similarly, the board must decide whether to use the information it got from governance training. The consultant has no direct influence and is not responsible for these decisions. When people do accept changes affecting organizational culture, they will sustain them long after the consultant is gone.

Note

1. A francolin is a large, partridge-like bird that is found in Africa and south Asia.

CHAPTER 6
Organizational assessment using proverbs

Conducting an organizational assessment is the first step in an organizational improvement process. Usually this involves raising awareness of what a healthy organization would look like and establishing where the organization is today in relation to the 'desired picture'. Establishing the gap between the ideal and the current situation is the essence of an organizational assessment.

The results of the assessment will point to the type of interventions needed and how these interventions should be carried out. This final chapter, in combination with assessment tools found in the appendices, will take the proverbs and lessons from the five previous chapters to a more immediately practicable level by providing a guided method by which organizations, leaders, and consultants can reflect on the implications of the proverbs for their own work. This assessment methodology has been developed and tested through numerous consultancies conducted by CADECD. When we began our practice, we faced two major challenges.

- Most of the organizational assessment tools in use were borrowed from the North.
- Most of the organizational assessment tools used in NGOs and CBOs were borrowed from the private business sector.

Our solution was to create the proverbs-based tools, which would enhance the communication of organizational issues in a language people from all types of organizations would easily understand. One version of the tool we developed is included in the Appendix.

What is an organizational assessment?

An organizational assessment is a checkup to determine the health of an organization. It focuses on the major aspects of organizational health reviewed in previous chapters:

- the sustainability of the organization and its services;

http://dx.doi.org/10.3362/9781780447599.007

- the skills, competencies, and capabilities of its people;
- the way people relate to one another and the way the organization relates to its stakeholders;
- the policies, procedures, and systems guiding decision-making processes;
- the strategy of the organization and its implementation;
- the vision and mission of the organization;
- the culture and values of the organization.

A healthy organization is one in which there is synchronicity among all these aspects and all are functioning properly. Only then can an organization boost its performance. This is also what distinguishes an organizational assessment from an evaluation or impact assessment. Many people confuse the two. An organizational assessment focuses on the internal aspects of the organization while an evaluation looks at the results it is producing. The two are related in that a sick organization cannot produce strong results.

The purpose of an organizational assessment

Conducting an organizational assessment is not an end in itself but a means toward an end. That end is developing an effective capacity-building plan to guide the organization. By 'effective', we mean a capacity-building plan that will actually be implemented. It is not enough to know how healthy or unhealthy an organization is if no action is undertaken to remedy the situation. The assessment becomes a benchmark against which to measure progress in improving organizational health.

The benefits of a self-assessment

Self-assessments have a number of special characteristics that enable them to benefit organizations in a number of ways.

- Self-assessment is a powerful diagnostic tool. It is an objective health check and it is a predictor for an organization's long-term success or failure.
- Self-assessment enables an organization to make objective comparisons with other organizations or its ideal.
- Self-assessment provides benchmarking opportunities and enables the organization to compare its performance over time

and across departments. This helps the organization to discover strengths and areas for improvement.

- Self-assessment provides a measure of the organization's capacity to meet the requirements and expectations of its clients and other stakeholders.
- Self-assessment can be a major motivation for process-focused improvement activities in priority areas. It can form a strong basis for strategic planning and leadership strengthening processes.

The organizational self-assessment process

The process of self-assessment goes through a number of stages.

Clarifying objectives and scope. The purpose of the assessment must be clarified at the beginning of the process. Most organizations use self-assessment as an organizational improvement tool. Assessments can be done with top management in strategic planning work or even at the lowest levels of the organization with the aim of identifying opportunities for improvement. The scope must specify whether the assessment will cover the whole organization or just some parts of it like departments or divisions.

Using the Proverbs Self-Assessment Tool for Organizations. There are many frameworks for self-assessment. The major strengths of the Proverbs Self-Assessment Tool are its strength and ability to add humour to otherwise sensitive organizational issues. The proverbs also are catalysts for generating dialogue among the people involved in the assessment. The rating enables the group to reach objective conclusions through consensus.

Forming the assessment team. Forming teams to do organizational assessments is better, because individuals may not have adequate in-depth knowledge of the organization and the tool being used. People may see the same things differently. Taking the different views into account enhances objectivity.

Planning the assessment. This stage looks at the issues of how the data and information will be collected and who will collect the data and information. The analysis of the data will also be planned at this stage. A time schedule is vital to guide this process.

Collecting the relevant data. Self-assessment must be as objective as possible. It must be based on fact and not opinion. The Proverbs Self-Assessment Tool works best in focus group discussions. To add objectivity, however, it may be necessary to triangulate the findings with other methods of collecting data, using different tools like questionnaires, individual interviews, document analysis, observation etc.

Analysing the data in a feedback workshop. This involves presenting the raw findings in a feedback workshop for participatory analysis, including distilling issues from the findings and clarifying where the findings were not clear. It works better when the feedback workshop is done at some quiet place away from the office to avoid interruptions and enhance concentration.

Action planning. After the participatory analysis, the next stage is to prioritize the identified issues and agree on the interventions that will be required to address them. (See the table in chapter 5 for a list of the major types of interventions.) The team also agrees on who will be responsible, when the interventions will happen, and what the indicators for achievement will be. The action plan can be used as a basis for measuring progress.

First-hand lessons for using African proverbs in OD work

CADECO has used African proverbs in its work in organizational assessment, strategic planning, team building, leadership development, board development and self-development interventions. We have also used African proverbs in working with a range of organizations including community-based organizations (CBOs), professional NGOs, churches and government departments. The following are key lessons learned through these experiences.

- When implementing proverbs-based self-assessment tools, the proverbs actually promote increased communication. The participants discuss their understanding of the proverbs, and apply them throughout the assessment process. In carrying out such self-assessments, we have also found it necessary to use an external facilitator to moderate the discussions and assessment process.

- It is critical to use the proverb that is most appropriate to an intervention or situation. Loosely using proverbs without a clear link to the issues may confuse the participants and disrupt the process.

- In training workshops, it is important to use proverbs sparingly to maximize their impact. Using too many proverbs may dilute their effectiveness. This also applies to the proverbs-based assessment tools. In a three-day team-building workshop, for example, we use up to three proverbs in an initial discussion session to elicit issues and insights for discussion. Thereafter, we only use them when they will add significant value and will promote insightful discussion more effectively than direct questions.

- It is important to use reflective questions in order to bring out insights from proverbs. Since proverbs may mean different things to different people in different contexts, the questions must be properly phrased and focused so as to elicit only those insights related to the issue at hand. In a self-development session for example, we might ask, 'What insights related to personal initiative can we learn from the following proverb?'

- Proverbs can also be used as reflective case studies by using the story upon which a proverb is based. A story is especially useful when dealing with complicated issues which may be difficult to communicate. For example, it is extremely challenging to teach organizational identity concepts. The use of a 'proverb case study' can easily help transcend such barriers. One story we have used in identity interventions is the one behind the proverb, 'An eaglet that does not know that it is an eagle may live like a chicken'. The story tells of an eagle egg that a farmer places amongst the eggs in a chicken coop. After hatching, the eagle is socialized into thinking it is a chicken and behaves as such until the day that an adult eagle flies overhead and screams at the eaglet. The young eagle instantly realizes that it does not belong among the chickens. Having never flown before, it miraculously takes flight to join the mother eagle. After relaying the story, we pose the following discussion questions: 'What does the story of the eaglet teach us as an organization?', 'How similar or different are we to the eaglet?', and 'What are we going to do in order to improve?'

- Proverbs must be used naturally and flexibly, and only when they add value to the process. If used mechanically, they may actually become a hindrance to the process. The power of proverbs, when used properly, is their invisibility as they facilitate the organizational development process without drawing attention to themselves. Development practitioners must not get so excited about the use of proverbs that they 'use crutches when they can walk on their own feet'.

Factors hindering effective use of organizational assessments

A number of factors hinder the effective use of organizational assessments.

Lack of ownership. One of the major observations we have made is that many organizations lack ownership of the organizational assessment process. Not many see value in an assessment and very few actually call to have one done. Many organizations undertake assessments at a donor's request as a means of getting money. Once the organization has the money, the motivation to implement the capacity-building plan wanes.

No culture of prevention. In most developing countries, there is not a strong tradition of having personal health checkups done regularly. People wait until they are really sick before seeking medical attention. The same thinking applies to the way organizations are run. As long as the pain is not felt, there is no reason for an assessment. It is conducted when the problem is serious, even though it could have been prevented earlier.

Fear of weaknesses. Many organizations are not willing to disclose their weaknesses. They look at assessments as a way of 'exposing' the organization. Such an attitude makes people reluctant and not authentic during the actual assessment process.

Lack of donor support. The end product of an organizational assessment is a capacity-building plan. Building the capacity of an organization is a long-term process and requires a long-term commitment. However, many donors are not enthusiastic about supporting organizations in this way and for that long. The paradox is that many donors are concerned with improving organizational performance without thinking about what produces that performance. Capacity building requires money. While not all capacity-building interventions require money, without financial support the plan may not be fully implemented and the health of the organization may not be improved.

Inattention to process. Lack of a process orientation among organizational change agents is another major hindrance to the effective use of organizational assessments. Many consultants still believe that acquiring money and providing training can solve all organizational problems. 'To the man with only a hammer in his toolkit, all problems look like nails.' Similarly, consultants often try to fix all problems with training. Training without long-term process interventions cannot resolve most deep-rooted problems organizations face. Trainings alone may produce superficial and short-lived results.

Not investing adequate time. Organizations working in challenging environments are often overwhelmed by the magnitude of the need they see. As a result, they end up getting caught up in a culture of 'busyness' that takes up all their time, leaving none for internal reflection and learning. In this case, no time is left for using the organizational assessments or implementing the capacity-building plan.

No monitoring systems. Many organizations lack effective monitoring and evaluation systems at both executive and board levels. The problem is more serious at the board level. Without effective monitoring and evaluation systems, organizations are not able to objectively assess their progress. This is complicated by the fact that most monitoring and evaluation systems are only concerned with the organization's performance and not its internal health. The assessment is forgotten and not valued.

Poor leadership. All the above factors are tied to the problem of absent visionary and effective leadership. Leaders who cannot see that the long-term performance and success of an organization is tied to its internal health will not value organizational assessments and their implementation.

While much more can be said on the process and benefits of self-assessment, there are other works much more suited to that purpose. With the overview provided in this chapter, we invite you to turn to the assessment tools and engage more deeply with the wisdom of the proverbs in this book.

There are a number of ways to use the organizational assessment tool. A fully facilitated group assessment guided by an external OD consultant, will likely provide the richest insight and the most complete picture of the organization. However, a quicker assessment can be conducted internally with self-reflection and response. Organizations may consider using the assessment as a lead-in to a strategic planning process or as an organizational strengthening activity on its own. The assessment tool can be adapted and proverbs and concepts added or deleted to make them relevant to your situation.

The leadership and consultant assessments are intended to be used more as individual self-reflection tools. Leaders and consultants should regularly find time to reflect on how they are performing their work and exhibiting the traits recommended by the proverbs in this book. This will serve to sharpen their overall skills and enable them to contribute more effectively to the organizations they serve.

All of the assessments are meant to 'create noise', and 'help scare the animals out of hiding'. Do not fear this. Instead, take it as an opportunity to sharpen your tools, to dig deeper into your identity and culture and to ensure the health and sustainability of an organization that can continue into the future to bring about meaningful change in its community.

Appendix

Sample diagnostic instruments

Proverbs self-assessment tool for organizations

0 <We do not experience this in our organization

├─────────┼─────────┼─────────┼─────────┤

We strongly experience or observe this in our organization> 5

REFLECTION PROVERBS	RATING (0-5)	EXPLANATION
LEADERSHIP AND VISION		
How clear and well-shared is the vision of the organization? • What the eyes have seen the heart cannot forget. • You can only jump over a ditch if you have seen it from afar.		
How effective is the leadership role in this organization? • An army of sheep led by a lion would defeat an army of lions led by a sheep. • When kings lose direction, they become servants.		
How approachable are our leaders? • The path to the chief's house does not grow grass.		
How do the leadership styles being practiced in this organization meet the different leadership needs of the organization? • When the beat of the drum changes, so must the step of the dance.		
How well does the organization develop its leadership for current and future needs in the areas of: *Effective time management?* • Time never goes back.		

http://dx.doi.org/10.3362/9781780447599.008

REFLECTION PROVERBS	RATING (0-5)	EXPLANATION
Concentrating and focusing on high leverage efforts and activities? • At the crossroads, you cannot go in both directions at the same time.		
Leadership succession? • When a reed dries up, another one grows in its place. *Building integrity?* • A crab's daughters cannot walk differently from their mother. • Character is like pregnancy, you cannot hide it for long. *Widening personal and organizational exposure?* • To one who has never traveled, a small garden is a big forest. • The eyes that have seen an ocean cannot be satisfied by a mere lagoon.		
STRATEGY		
How well is the organization using its cutting edge against competition? • A mother of twins must sleep on her back.		
How well does the leadership balance long-term and short-term needs in its thinking and planning in this organization? • Since men have learned to shoot without missing, birds have learned to fly without perching. • There is no such a thing as bad weather, only bad clothing.		
How consciously and proactively does the organization learn from what is happening in its task environment? • If you can bear the hissing of a snake, do not complain when you are bitten.		
How conscious are people in the organization about the changes in the state of the internal health of the organization over time? • An egg does not go bad in one day.		

REFLECTION PROVERBS	RATING (0-5)	EXPLANATION
In addressing its issues, is the organization addressing real issues or only symptoms? • If you cut a piece of a liana creeper without removing the roots, it will continue to creep.		
How effective are the organization's strategies in terms of: *Identifying and utilizing leverage?* • A hunter with one arrow does not shoot with a careless aim. • If you are not pretty, know how to sing.		
Being focused for concentration? • When you are at the crossroads, you cannot go in both directions at the same time. *Being realistic about the organization's capacity to carry out its work?* • What a duck has failed to pick, a chicken cannot. *Recognizing that organizational growth and development takes time?* • There are no shortcuts to the top of a palm tree. • Even the biggest rooster that crows the loudest was once upon a time just an egg. • Little by little the snail reached its destination. *Implementing strategies?* • A lazy man's farm is the breeding ground for snakes. • Pray for a good harvest, but keep on hoeing. • Success is a ladder that cannot be climbed with hands in your pocket.		
ROLES AND RESPONSIBILITIES		
How well are the roles and responsibilities defined and respected in this organization? • Two roosters do not crow in the same pen.		

REFLECTION PROVERBS	RATING (0-5)	EXPLANATION
• Two fingers cannot enter into one nostril. • A cat in his house has the teeth of a lion. • If the sun says it is more powerful than the moon, then let it come and shine at night.		
How well is conflict managed in this organization? • You cannot kill the rat when it is sitting on your clay pot. • There is no venom like that of the tongue. • When elephants fight, it is the grass that suffers.		
How strong is the team spirit in this organization? • No matter how powerful a man, he cannot make rain fall on his farm alone. • One person cannot move a mountain. • Friendship is adding value. • The man who eats alone dies alone. • United we are rock and divided we are sand.		
How well do individuals and departments work together and how well does the organization work together with other organizations? • When cobwebs unite, they can tie up a lion.		
How well are power and politics exercised in the organization? • Those who live in peace work for it. • We make war so that we can live in peace. • Negotiate with your enemy while you are a strong and formidable force, and he will always fear and respect you; but negotiate at the brink of defeat, and he will trample you down.		

REFLECTION PROVERBS	RATING (0-5)	EXPLANATION
POLICIES, SYSTEMS, AND PROCEDURES		
How effective are the rules and regulations in the organization? • Rules are stronger than an individual's power. • There can be no village without rules.		
How effective is the process of formulating policies, systems, and procedures? • A chief should not make rules alone. • A chief should not make rules when he is angry.		
CULTURE		
How conscious are the people of the effect of their behaviors and attitudes on the effectiveness of the organization? • The owner of a smell does not notice it. • You cannot tell the quality of a fig fruit by its outside appearance.		
How clear is the identity of the organization both to insiders and other stakeholders? • Because of his double identity, the bat was never buried. • The person you know during day time should also be recognizable at night.		
How free are people to express their real feelings in this organization? • When you are hunting, animals will only come out when you make noise. • The man who kicks his old friend for warning him that the path he has chosen is disastrous can only be headed for trouble. • An antelope cannot drink water when a hunting dog is chasing it.		
How are people judged in this organization? What is given value? • Do not be quick to insult the madman who frequently comes to your doorstep. He may become your mother's husband.		

REFLECTION PROVERBS	RATING (0-5)	EXPLANATION
How transparent are processes and the way decisions are made in this organization? • You can't hide the smoke when the house is burning.		
How well does the organization balance action and learning? • When the lion runs and looks back, it is not that he is afraid, rather he is trying to see the distance he has covered.		
How committed are employees to stay on in this organization? • A bird in hand is worth two in the bush. • Grass may be greener on the other side, but it is just as difficult to cut. • A happy man marries the woman he loves; a happier man loves the woman he marries.		
Is the organization creating an empowering organizational culture? • Constructive arguments build a village. • A visitor brings a sharper razor blade. • A visitor sees more in an hour than the hosts in a year.		
SUSTAINABILITY		
How sustainable is the organization in its client, organizational, and financial aspects? • Money is not everything. • Your own farm implements are more important than your mother and father. • If you eat all your harvest, you won't have seed for tomorrow. • Recognition comes with having one's own possessions. • A borrowed axe doesn't last. • In your good times, prepare for bad times, and in your bad limes, prepare for good times. • A healthy chick comes from a healthy egg.		

Self-reflection tool for leaders

This tool can be used to assess a leader's effectiveness. It can be used in two main ways.

Periodic personal reflection. By periodically and objectively assessing himself or herself against the aspects in the tool, a leader can maintain his or her progress. This can form the basis for self-development initiatives and developing one's practice.

Periodic interpersonal reflection. Where the leader has a speaking partner or a support group, the tool can be used for receiving and giving feedback on his or her own development.

REFLECTION PROVERBS	RATING (0-5)	EXPLANATION
How effectively am I helping people to commit to the vision of the organization? • What the eyes have seen, the heart cannot forget. • You can only jump over a ditch if you have seen it from afar.		
How effective is my leadership role in this organization? • An army of sheep led by a lion would defeat an army of lions led by a sheep. • When kings lose direction, they become servants.		
How do the leadership styles I practice in the organization meet the different leadership needs of the organization? • When the beat of the drum changes, so must the step of the dance.		
How well do I develop organizational leadership for current and future needs in the areas of: • Effective time management? • Time never goes back.		
Concentrating and focusing on high leverage efforts and activities? • At the crossroads, you cannot go in both directions at the same time.		
Leadership succession? • When a reed dries up, another one grows in its place.		

REFLECTION PROVERBS	RATING (0-5)	EXPLANATION
Building integrity? • A crab's daughters cannot walk differently from their mother. • Character is like pregnancy, you cannot hide it for long.		
Widening personal and organizational exposure? • To one who has never travelled, a small garden is a big forest. • The eyes that have seen an ocean cannot be satisfied by a mere lagoon.		

Self-reflection tool for consultants

This tool can help consultants to assess the effectiveness of their practices. It can be used in two main ways.

Periodic personal reflection. By periodically and objectively assessing himself or herself against the aspects in the tool, the consultant can maintain his or her progress. This can form the basis for self-development initiatives and developing one's practice.

Periodic interpersonal reflection. Where the consultant has a speaking partner or a support group, the tool can be used for receiving and giving feedback on his or her development.

REFLECTION PROVERBS	RATING (0-5)	EXPLANATION
PERSONAL TRANSFORMATION How conscious am I about my own need for personal transformation before intervening into the client system? • *A changed place cannot transform an individual but a transformed individual can change a place.*		
MARKETING CONSULTING SERVICES How well am I marketing my services? • *Good merchandise sells itself.*		
OBJECTIVITY IN INTERVENING How objective am I when listening to parties holding different views in the client system? • *Taking action based on one person's view is provoking wasps in a nest.*		
OBSERVATION In addition to what they tell me, how deep is my observation? • *To see a snail's eyes one must be very patient.*		
THE QUALITY OF QUESTIONS How good is the quality of my questions in soliciting real issues and in moving the client organization from where it is stuck? • *The hand that tied the lion knows best how to untie it.*		

REFLECTION PROVERBS	RATING (0-5)	EXPLANATION
INTERVENING IN ORGANIZATIONAL CULTURE How well am I using my status as a 'visitor' to see more and give more constructive feedback to the client? • *A guest sees more in an hour than the host in a year.*		
SUPPORT SYSTEMS How realistic am I about my capabilities and the need for a coach, mentor, and/or speaking partner? • *What elders see while sitting, the young may not see while standing.* • *No matter how sharp a knife is it cannot cut itself.*		
EMPATHY How well do I make people in the client organization understand that change is their responsibility and that I am just a facilitator? • *The sympathizer cannot mourn more than the bereaved.*		
ENSURING OWNERSHIP OF INTERVENTIONS How well do I put in place mechanisms to ensure ownership and sustained change after I leave the client? • *You can take the goat to the river but you cannot force it to drink the water.*		

References

Achebe, C. (1983) *The Trouble with Nigeria*, London: Heinemann.

BBC Network Africa (2002) *The Wisdom of Africa*, London: BBC World Service.

Blunt, P. and Jones, M. (1992) *Managing Organizations in Africa*, Berlin: De Gruyter Studies in Organization.

Chakanza, J. (2000) *The Wisdom of the People: 2000 Chinyanja Proverbs*, Blantyre: Christian Literature Association of Malawi (CLAIM).

Dainty, P. and Anderson, M. (1996) *The Capable Executive: Effective Performance in Senior Management*, London: Macmillan Press.

Drucker, P. (1955) *Managing for Results*, Oxford: Butterworth-Heinemann.

Drucker, P. (1967) *The Effective Executive*, Oxford: Butterworth-Heinemann.

Drucker, P. (1974) *Management: Tasks, Responsibilities, Practices*, Oxford: Butterworth-Heinemann.

Drucker, P. (1980) *Managing in Turbulent Times*, Oxford: Butterworth-Heinemann.

Drucker, P. (1990) *Managing the Non-Profit Organization*, Oxford: Butterworth-Heinemann.

Drucker, P. (1991) *Managing for the Future*, Oxford: Butterworth-Heinemann.

Fowler, A. (1996) *Institutional Development and NGOs in Africa: Policy Perceptions for European Development Agencies*, Oxford: INTRAC.

French, W.L. and Bell, C. (1995) *Organizational Development: Behavioral Science Interventions for Organization Improvement*, 5th edn, New Jersey: Prentice-Hall Inc.

Hammer, M. and Champy, J. (2001) *Reengineering the Corporation: A Manifesto for Business Revolution*, London: Nicholas Brealy Publishing.

Handy, C. (1985) *Understanding Organizations*, London: Penguin Group.

Handy, C. (1998) *Understanding Voluntary Organizations*, Hammondsworth: Penguin.

Howell, W. (1976) *Essentials of Industrial and Organizational Psychology*, Homewood, Illinois: Dorsey Press.

Kumakanga, S. (1975) Nzeru za Kale [*Wisdom of Ancient Times*], Blantyre: Longman.

Jones, M.L. and Blunt, P. (1993) 'Organizational development and change in Africa', *International Journal of Public Administration* 16 (11): 1735–65 <http://dx.doi.org/10.1080/01900699308524871>.

Johnson, S. and Wilson, L. (1984) *The One Minute Sales Person*, Londu. Harper Collins.

Johnson, H. and Wilson. G. (1999) 'Institutional sustainability as learning', *Development in Practice*, 9 (1–2): 43–55 <http://dx.doi.org/10.1080/09614529953205>.

Livegoed, B. (1969) *Managing the Developing Organization*, Oxford: Blackwell.

Livegoed, B. (1973) *The Developing Organization*, London: Tavistock.

Lynch, J. (1995) *Customer Loyalty and Success*, London: Macmillan.

Maathai, W. (1995) *Bottlenecks of Development in Africa*, Beijing: United Nations Centre for Human Settlement (Habitat).

Mason, J. (1965) *How to Build Your Management Skills*, New York: McGraw-Hill Book Company.

Maxwell, J. (1998) *The 21 Irrefutable Laws of Leadership*, Florida: African Nazarine Publications.

Mbeki, T. (1998) *The African Renaissance: South Africa and the World*, Tokyo: United Nations University.

Mbeki, T. (1998) *Mahube: the Dawning of Dawn*, Braamfontein: Skotaville Media.

Mbigi, L. (1995) *Ubuntu – The Spirit of African Transformation Management*, Randburg: Knowledge Resource.

Michongwe, G. (2001) *Ethics of the Teaching Profession*, Zomba: Malawi Institute of Education.

Mulle, H. (2001) 'Challenges to African governance and civil society', in *Public Administration and Development*, 21: 71–6.

Nangoli, M. (1986) *No More Lies about Africa: Here's the Truth from an African*, New Jersey: Heritage Publishers.

Porter, L. and Tanner, S. (1998) *Assessing Business Excellence*, Oxford: Butterworth-Heinemann.

Sampson, A. (1999) *Mandela: The Authorised Biography*, London: Harper Collins Publishers.

Sahley, C. (1995) *Strengthening the Capacity of NGOs: Cases of Small Enterprises Development in Africa*, Oxford: INTRAC.

Senge, P. (1990) *The Fifth Discipline: The Art and Practice of the Learning Organization*, New York: Doubleday.

Smillie, I. (1995) *Alms Bazaar: Altruism Under Fire – Non-profit Organizations and International Development*, Rugby, UK: Practical Action Publishing.

Tengey, W. (1991) *A Guide to Promote Rural Self-Reliant Development (a Ghana Experience)*, Accra: Africa Centre for Human Development.

Vincent, F. (1995) *Alternative Financing of Third World Development Organizations and NGOs*, Geneva: IRED.

Waiguchu, J. (2001) *Management of Organizations in Africa: A Handbook and Reference*, London: Quorum Books.